PLAYS BY PETER SHAFFER

Five Finger Exercise   1959

The Private Ear & The Public Eye   1962

The Royal Hunt of the Sun   1965

Black Comedy & White Lies   1969

Equus   1973

Shrivings   1974

EQUUS
AND
SHRIVINGS

EQUUS

AND

SHRIVINGS

Two Plays by

PETER SHAFFER

New York

ATHENEUM

1974

EQUUS

For PAUL
with love

A NOTE ON THE BOOK

What appears in this book is a description of the first production of *Equus* at the National Theatre in July 1973. In making this description, I am partly satisfying myself, but also partly bowing to demand.

When people buy the published text of a new play, they mostly want to recall the experience they received in the theatre. That experience is composed, of course, not merely of the words they heard, but the gestures they saw, and the lighting, and the look of the thing.

There are, however, evils attendant on this sort of description. It can imprison a play in one particular stylisation. Just as seriously, it can do a real injustice to the original Director, by incorporating his ideas without truly acknowledging them. Worse, if the Director is as inventive as John Dexter, it can actually seem to minimise those ideas, just by flatly setting down on paper what was far from flat on the stage, and listing inexpressively, details of his work which, in accumulation, became deeply expressive.

Dexter directs powerfully through suggestion. Into the theatrical spaces he contrives, flows the communal imagination of an audience. He enables it to charge the action of a play with electric life. He is a master of gesture and of economy. Aesthetically, his founding fathers are Noh Drama and Berthold Brecht: the plain plank; the clear light; the great pleasure in a set-piece. I do not mean by this that he would ever direct a single minute of physical action which detracted from the meaning of a play, or in some grand visual sense subverted it – he sharply dislikes effect isolated from context – but he is naturally and rightly drawn to plays which demand elaborate physical actions to complete them.

The Royal Hunt of the Sun and *Black Comedy*, both of which he directed, are such pieces: and so is *Equus*. Their visual action is to me as much a part of the play as the dialogue. I suppose my head has always been full of images. The gold masks staring hopefully and then in gathering despair at the sky, at the end of *The Royal Hunt of the Sun*, had been part of my imagination ever since I first saw a Peruvian funeral mask with its elongated eyes and red-smeared cheeks. Brindsley Miller in the lit-up darkness of *Black Comedy*, slowly moving the spiky legs of a Regency chair one inch before the innocent face of his spinster neighbour, had tiptoed that very journey in my head as I sat at my desk. But such images, like the Field of Ha-ha in *Equus* with its mist and nettles, still have to be externalised. In John Dexter's courageous and precise staging, they acquire a vibrant and unforgettable life.

While I am confessing debts, let me mention John Napier who created the tough, bright masks of horsedom; Andy Phillips who lit them superbly; and above all, Claude Chagrin, who animated them. She created, with the help of six human actors, a stable of Superhorses to stalk through the mind.

Finally, out of a fine company I must set down the names of three actors who made the first performance of this play live with a very special intensity. Alec McCowen's *Dysart* touched audiences deeply with its dry agony. Peter Firth's *Alan* left them sighing with admiration. Nicholas Clay's horse, *Nugget* was, quite simply, unforgettable.

Rehearsing a play is making the word flesh. Publishing a play is reversing the process. I can only hope this book is not too unjust to these brilliant people.

P.S.

A NOTE ON THE PLAY

One weekend over two years ago, I was driving with a friend through bleak countryside. We passed a stable. Suddenly he was reminded by it of an alarming crime which he had heard about recently at a dinner party in London. He knew only one horrible detail, and his complete mention of it could barely have lasted a minute – but it was enough to arouse in me an intense fascination.

The act had been committed several years before by a highly disturbed young man. It had deeply shocked a local bench of magistrates. It lacked, finally, any coherent explanation.

A few months later my friend died. I could not verify what he had said, or ask him to expand it. He had given me no name, no place, and no time. I don't think he knew them. All I possessed was his report of a dreadful event, and the feeling it engendered in me. I knew very strongly that I wanted to interpret it in some entirely personal way. I had to create a mental world in which the deed could be made comprehensible.

Every person and incident in *Equus* is of my own invention, save the crime itself: and even that I modified to accord with what I feel to be acceptable theatrical proportion. I am grateful now that I have never received confirmed details of the real story, since my concern has been more and more with a different kind of exploration.

I have been lucky, in doing final work on the play, to have enjoyed the advice and expert comment of a distinguished child psychiatrist. Through him I have tried to keep things real in a more naturalistic sense. I have also come to perceive that psychiatrists are an immensely varied breed, professing immensely varied methods and techniques. Martin Dysart is simply one doctor in one hospital. I must take responsibility for him, as I do for his patient.

THE SET

A square of wood set on a circle of wood.

The square resembles a railed boxing ring. The rail, also of wood, encloses three sides. It is perforated on each side by an opening. Under the rail are a few vertical slats, as if in a fence. On the downstage side there is no rail. The whole square is set on ball bearings, so that by slight pressure from actors standing round it on the circle, it can be made to turn round smoothly by hand.

On the square are set three little plain benches, also of wood. They are placed parallel with the rail, against the slats, but can be moved out by the actors to stand at right angles to them.

Set into the floor of the square, and flush with it, is a thin metal pole, about a yard high. This can be raised out of the floor, to stand upright. It acts as a support for the actor playing Nugget, when he is ridden.

In the area outside the circle stand benches. Two downstage left and right, are curved to accord with the circle. The left one is used by Dysart as a listening and observing post when he is out of the square, and also by Alan as his hospital bed. The right one is used by Alan's parents, who sit side by side on it. (Viewpoint is from the main body of the audience.)

Further benches stand upstage, and accommodate the other actors. All the cast of *Equus* sits on stage the entire evening. They get up to perform their scenes, and return when they are done to their places around the set. They are witnesses, assistants – and especially a Chorus.

Upstage, forming a backdrop to the whole, are tiers of seats in the fashion of a dissecting theatre, formed into two railed-off blocks, pierced by a central tunnel. In these blocks sit members of the audience. During the play, Dysart addresses them directly from time to time, as he addresses the main body of the theatre. No other actor ever refers to them.

To left and right, downstage, stand two ladders on which are suspended horse masks.

The colour of all benches is olive green.

Above the stage hangs a battery of lights, set in a huge metal ring. Light cues, in this version, will be only of the most general description.

CHARACTERS

MARTIN DYSART, *a psychiatrist*
ALAN STRANG
FRANK STRANG, *his father*
DORA STRANG, *his mother*
HESTHER SALOMON, *a magistrate*
JILL MASON
HARRY DALTON, *a stable owner*
A YOUNG HORSEMAN
A NURSE

SIX ACTORS – *including the Young Horseman, who also plays Nugget – appear as Horses.*

The main action of the play takes place in Rokeby Psychiatric Hospital in Southern England.

The time is the present.

The play is divided into numbered scenes, indicating a change of time or locale or mood. The action, however, is continuous.

THE HORSES

The actors wear track-suits of chestnut velvet. On their feet are light strutted hooves, about four inches high, set on metal horse-shoes. On their hands are gloves of the same colour. On their heads are tough masks made of alternating bands of silver wire and leather: their eyes are outlined by leather blinkers. The actors' own heads are seen beneath them: no attempt should be made to conceal them.

Any literalism which could suggest the cosy familiarity of a domestic animal – or worse, a pantomime horse – should be avoided. The actors should never crouch on all fours, or even bend forward. They must always – except on the one occasion where Nugget is ridden – stand upright, as if the body of the horse extended invisibly behind them. Animal effect must be created entirely mimetically, through the use of legs, knees, neck, face, and the turn of the head which can move the mask above it through all the gestures of equine wariness and pride. Great care must also be taken that the masks are put on before the audience with very precise timing – the actors watching each other, so that the masking has an exact and ceremonial effect.

THE CHORUS

References are made in the text to the Equus Noise. I have in mind a choric effect, made by all the actors sitting round up-stage, and composed of humming, thumping, and stamping – though never of neighing or whinnying. This Noise heralds or illustrates the presence of Equus the God.

Equus was first presented by The National Theatre at The Old Vic Theatre on July 26, 1973, with the following cast:

MARTIN DYSART	Alec McCowen
NURSE	Louie Ramsay
HESTHER SALOMON	Gillian Barge
ALAN STRANG	Peter Firth
FRANK STRANG	Alan MacNaughtan
DORA STRANG	Jeanne Watts
HORSEMAN	Nicholas Clay
HARRY DALTON	David Healy
JILL MASON	Doran Godwin
and	

Neil Cunningham, David Graham, David Kincaid, Maggie Riley, Rosalind Shanks, Veronica Sowerby, Harry Waters

PRODUCTION	John Dexter
DESIGN	John Napier
MUSIC	Marc Wilkinson
LIGHTING	Andy Phillips
MOVEMENT	Claude Chagrin
ASSISTANT TO THE PRODUCER	Kenneth Mackintosh
STAGE MANAGER	Diana Boddington
DEPUTY STAGE MANAGERS	Phil Robins
	Tony Walters
ASSISTANT STAGE MANAGERS	Elizabeth Markham
	Terry Oliver

ACT ONE

I

Darkness.
Silence.
Dim light up on the square. In a spotlight stands Alan
Strang, a lean boy of seventeen, in sweater and jeans. In
front of him, the horse Nugget. Alan's pose represents a
contour of great tenderness: his head is pressed against
the shoulder of the horse, his hands stretching up to fondle
its head. The horse in turn nuzzles his neck.
The flame of a cigarette lighter jumps in the dark. Lights
come up slowly on the circle. On the left bench, downstage,
Martin Dysart, smoking. A man in his mid-forties.

DYSART: With one particular horse, called Nugget, he embraces. The animal digs its sweaty brow into his cheek, and
they stand in the dark for an hour – like a necking couple.
And of all nonsensical things – I keep thinking about the
horse! Not the boy: the horse, and what it may be trying to
do. I keep seeing that huge head kissing him with its chained
mouth. Nudging through the metal some desire absolutely
irrelevant to filling its belly or propagating its own kind.
What desire could that be? Not to stay a horse any longer?
Not to remain reined up for ever in those particular genetic
strings? Is it possible, at certain moments we cannot imagine,
a horse can add its sufferings together – the non-stop jerks
and jabs that are its daily life – and turn them into grief?
What use is grief to a horse?
Alan leads Nugget out of the square and they disappear
together up the tunnel, the horse's hooves scraping
delicately on the wood.
Dysart rises, and addresses both the large audience in the
theatre and the smaller one on stage.

17

You see, I'm lost. What use, I should be asking, are questions like these to an overworked psychiatrist in a provincial hospital? They're worse than useless: they are, in fact, subversive.

He enters the square. The light grows brighter.

The thing is, I'm desperate. You see, I'm wearing that horse's head myself. That's the feeling. All reined up in old language and old assumptions, straining to jump clean-hoofed on to a whole new track of being I only suspect is there. I can't see it, because my educated, average head is being held at the wrong angle. I can't jump because the bit forbids it, and my own basic force – my horsepower, if you like – is too little. The only thing I know for sure is this: a horse's head is finally unknowable to me. Yet I handle children's heads – which I must presume to be more complicated, at least in the area of my chief concern. . . . In a way, it has nothing to do with this boy. The doubts have been there for years, piling up steadily in this dreary place. It's only the extremity of this case that's made them active. I know that. The *extremity* is the point! All the same, whatever the reason, they are now, these doubts, not just vaguely worrying – but intolerable . . . I'm sorry. I'm not making much sense. Let me start properly: in order. It began one Monday last month, with Hesther's visit.

2.

The light gets warmer.
He sits. Nurse enters the square.

NURSE: Mrs Salomon to see you, Doctor.
DYSART: Show her in, please.

Nurse leaves and crosses to where Hesther sits.

Some days I blame Hesther. She brought him to me. But of course that's nonsense. What is he but a last straw? a last symbol? If it hadn't been him, it would have been the next patient, or the next. At least, I suppose so.

Hesther enters the square: a woman in her mid-forties.
HESTHER: Hallo, Martin.
Dysart rises and kisses her on the cheek.
DYSART: Madam Chairman! Welcome to the torture chamber!
HESTHER: It's good of you to see me right away.
DYSART: You're a welcome relief. Take a couch.
HESTHER: It's been a day?
DYSART: No – just a fifteen year old schizophrenic, and a girl of eight thrashed into catatonia by her father. Normal, really ... You're in a state.
HESTHER: Martin, this is the most shocking case I ever tried.
DYSART: So you said on the phone.
HESTHER: I mean it. My bench wanted to send the boy to prison. For life, if they could manage it. It took me two hours solid arguing to get him sent to you instead.
DYSART: Me?
HESTHER: I mean, to hospital.
DYSART: Now look, Hesther. Before you say anything else, I can take no more patients at the moment. I can't even cope with the ones I have.
HESTHER: You must.
DYSART: Why?
HESTHER: Because most people are going to be disgusted by the whole thing. Including doctors.
DYSART: May I remind you I share this room with two highly competent psychiatrists?
HESTHER: Bennett and Thoroughgood. They'll be as shocked as the public.
DYSART: That's an absolutely unwarrantable statement.
HESTHER: Oh, they'll be cool and exact. And underneath they'll be revolted, and immovably English. Just like my bench.
DYSART: Well, what am I? Polynesian?
HESTHER: You know exactly what I mean! ... [*pause*] Please, Martin. It's vital. You're this boy's only chance.
DYSART: Why? What's he done? Dosed some little girl's Pepsi with Spanish Fly? What could possibly throw your bench into two-hour convulsions?

19

HESTHER: He blinded six horses with a metal spike.
> *A long pause.*

DYSART: Blinded?

HESTHER: Yes.

DYSART: All at once, or over a period?

HESTHER: All on the same night.

DYSART: Where?

HESTHER: In a riding stable near Winchester. He worked there at weekends.

DYSART: How old?

HESTHER: Seventeen.

DYSART: What did he say in Court?

HESTHER: Nothing. He just sang.

DYSART: Sang?

HESTHER: Any time anyone asked him anything.
> *Pause.*

Please take him, Martin. It's the last favour I'll ever ask you.

DYSART: No, it's not.

HESTHER: No, it's not – and he's probably abominable. All I know is, he needs you badly. Because there really is nobody within a hundred miles of your desk who can handle him. And perhaps understand what this is about. Also ....

DYSART: What?

HESTHER: There's something very special about him.

DYSART: In what way?

HESTHER: Vibrations.

DYSART: You and your vibrations.

HESTHER: They're quite startling. You'll see.

DYSART: When does he get here?

HESTHER: Tomorrow morning. Luckily there was a bed in Neville Ward. I know this is an awful imposition, Martin. Frankly I didn't know what else to do.
> *Pause.*

DYSART: Can you come in and see me on Friday?

HESTHER: Bless you!

DYSART: If you come after work I can give you a drink. Will 6.30 be all right?

HESTHER: You're a dear. You really are.

DYSART: Famous for it.
HESTHER: Goodbye.
DYSART: By the way, what's his name?
HESTHER: Alan Strang.
She leaves and returns to her seat.
DYSART: [to audience] What did I expect of him? Very little,
I promise you. One more dented little face. One more
adolescent freak. The usual unusual. One great thing about
being in the adjustment business: you're never short of
customers.
*Nurse comes down the tunnel, followed by Alan. She
enters the square.*
NURSE: Alan Strang, Doctor.
The boy comes in.
DYSART: Hallo. My name's Martin Dysart. I'm pleased to
meet you.
He puts out his hand. Alan does not respond in any way.
That'll be all, Nurse, thank you.

3.

Nurse goes out and back to her place.
Dysart sits, opening a file.
So: did you have a good journey? I hope they gave you
lunch at least. Not that there's much to choose between a
British Rail meal and one here.
Alan stands staring at him.
DYSART: Won't you sit down?
Pause. He does not. Dysart consults his file.
Is this your full name? Alan Strang?
Silence.
And you're seventeen. Is that right? Seventeen? ... Well?
ALAN [*singing low*] Double your pleasure,
Double your fun
With Doublemint, Doublemint
Doublemint gum.
DYSART: [*unperturbed*] Now, let's see. You work in an elec-

21

trical shop during the week. You live with your parents, and your father's a printer. What sort of things does he print?

ALAN: [*singing louder*] Double your pleasure
Double your fun
With Doublemint, Doublemint
Doublemint gum.

DYSART: I mean does he do leaflets and calendars? Things like that?

The boy approaches him, hostile.

ALAN: [*singing*] Try the taste of Martini
The most beautiful drink in the world.
It's the right one –
The bright one –
That's Martini!

DYSART: I wish you'd sit down, if you're going to sing. Don't you think you'd be more comfortable?

Pause.

ALAN: [*singing*] There's only one T in Typhoo!
In packets and in teabags too.
Any way you make it, you'll find it's true:
There's only one T in Typhoo!

DYSART: [*appreciatively*] Now that's a good song. I like it better than the other two. Can I hear that one again?

Alan starts away from him, and sits on the upstage bench.

ALAN: [*singing*] Double your pleasure
Double your fun
With Doublemint, Doublemint
Doublemint gum.

DYSART: [*smiling*] You know I was wrong. I really do think that one's better. It's got such a catchy tune. Please do that one again.

Silence. The boy glares at him.

I'm going to put you in a private bedroom for a little while. There are one or two available, and they're rather more pleasant than being in a ward. Will you please come and see me tomorrow? . . . [*He rises*] By the way, which parent is it who won't allow you to watch television? Mother or father? Or is it both? [*calling out of the door*] Nurse!

22

Alan stares at him. Nurse comes in.

NURSE: Yes, Doctor?

DYSART: Take Strang here to Number Three, will you? He's moving in there for a while.

NURSE: Very good, Doctor.

DYSART: [*to Alan*] You'll like that room. It's nice.

The boy sits staring at Dysart.
Dysart returns the stare.

NURSE: Come along, young man. This way. . . . I said this way, please.

Reluctantly Alan rises and goes to Nurse, passing dangerously close to Dysart, and out through the left door. Dysart looks after him, fascinated.

4.

Nurse and patient move on to the circle, and walk downstage to the bench where the doctor first sat, which is to serve also as Alan's bed.

NURSE: Well now: isn't this nice? You're lucky to be in here, you know, rather than the ward. That ward's a noisy old place.

ALAN: [*singing*] Let's go where you wanna go – Texaco!

NURSE: [*contemplating him*] I hope you're not going to make a nuisance of yourself. You'll have a much better time of it here, you know, if you behave yourself.

ALAN: Fuck off.

NURSE: [*tight*] That's the bell there. The lav's down the corridor.

She leaves him, and goes back to her place.
Alan lies down.

5.

Dysart stands in the middle of the square and addresses the audience. He is agitated.

DYSART: That night, I had this very explicit dream. In it I'm a chief priest in Homeric Greece. I'm wearing a wide gold mask, all noble and bearded, like the so-called Mask of Agamemnon found at Mycenae. I'm standing by a thick round stone and holding a sharp knife. In fact, I'm officiating at some immensely important ritual sacrifice, on which depends the fate of the crops or of a military expedition. The sacrifice is a herd of children: about five hundred boys and girls. I can see them stretching away in a long queue, right across the plain of Argos. I know it's Argos because of the red soil. On either side of me stand two assistant priests, wearing masks as well: lumpy, pop-eyed masks, such as also were found at Mycenae. They are enormously strong, these other priests, and absolutely tireless. As each child steps forward, they grab it from behind and throw it over the stone. Then, with a surgical skill which amazes even me, I fit in the knife and slice elegantly down to the navel, just like a seamstress following a pattern. I part the flaps, sever the inner tubes, yank them out and throw them hot and steaming on to the floor. The other two then study the pattern they make, as if they were reading hieroglyphics. It's obvious to me that I'm tops as chief priest. It's this unique talent for carving that has got me where I am. The only thing is, unknown to them, I've started to feel distinctly nauseous. And with each victim, it's getting worse. My face is going green behind the mask. Of course, I redouble my efforts to look professional – cutting and snipping for all I'm worth: mainly because I know that if ever those two assistants so much as glimpse my distress – and the implied doubt that this repetitive and smelly work is doing any social good at all – I will be the next across the stone. And then, of course – the damn mask begins to slip. The priests both turn and look at it – it slips some more – they see the green sweat running down my face – their gold pop-eyes suddenly fill up with blood – they tear the knife out of my hand . . . and I wake up.

24

6.

Hesther enters the square. Light grows warmer.

HESTHER: That's the most indulgent thing I ever heard.

DYSART: You think?

HESTHER: Please don't be ridiculous. You've done the most superb work with children. You must know that.

DYSART: Yes, but do the children?

HESTHER: Really!

DYSART: I'm sorry.

HESTHER: So you should be.

DYSART: I don't know why you listen. It's just professional menopause. Everyone gets it sooner or later. Except you.

HESTHER: Oh, of course. I feel totally fit to be a magistrate all the time.

DYSART: No, you don't – but then that's you feeling unworthy to fill a job. I feel the job is unworthy to fill me.

HESTHER: Do you seriously?

DYSART: More and more. I'd like to spend the next ten years wandering very slowly around the *real* Greece . . . Anyway, all this dream nonsense is your fault.

HESTHER: Mine?

DYSART: It's that lad of yours who started it off. Do you know it's his face I saw on every victim across the stone?

HESTHER: Strang?

DYSART: He has the strangest stare I ever met.

HESTHER. Yes.

DYSART: It's exactly like being accused. Violently accused. But what of? . . . Treating him is going to be unsettling. Especially in my present state. His singing was direct enough. His speech is more so.

HESTHER: [*surprised*] He's talking to you, then?

DYSART: Oh yes. It took him two more days of commercials, and then he snapped. Just like that – I suspect it has something to do with his nightmares.

Nurse walks briskly round the circle, a blanket over her arm, a clipboard of notes in her hand.

25

HESTHER: He has nightmares?

DYSART: Bad ones.

NURSE: We had to give him a sedative or two, Doctor. Last night it was exactly the same.

DYSART: [to Nurse] What does he do? Call out?

NURSE: [to desk] A lot of screaming, Doctor.

DYSART: [to Nurse] Screaming?

NURSE: One word in particular.

DYSART: [to Nurse] You mean a special word?

NURSE: Over and over again. [Consulting clipboard] It sounds like 'Ek'.

HESTHER: Ek?

NURSE: Yes, Doctor. Ek. . . . 'Ek!' he goes. 'Ek!'

HESTHER: How weird.

NURSE: When I woke him up he clung to me like he was going to break my arm.

She stops at Alan's bed. He is sitting up. She puts the blanket over him, and returns to her place.

DYSART: And then he burst in – just like that – without knocking or anything. Fortunately, I didn't have a patient with me.

ALAN: [Jumping up] Dad!

HESTHER: What?

DYSART: The answer to a question I'd asked him two days before. Spat out with the same anger as he sang the commercials.

HESTHER: Dad what?

ALAN: Who hates telly.

He lies downstage on the circle, as if watching television.

HESTHER: You mean his dad forbids him to watch?

DYSART: Yes.

ALAN: It's a dangerous drug.

HESTHER: Oh, really!

Frank stands up and enters the scene downstage on the circle. A man in his fifties.

FRANK: [to Alan] It may not look like that, but that's what it is. Absolutely fatal mentally, if you receive my meaning.

Dora follows him on. She is also middle-aged.

DORA: That's a little extreme, dear, isn't it?

FRANK: You sit in front of that thing long enough, you'll become stupid for life – like most of the population. [to Alan] The thing is, it's a swiz. It seems to be offering you something, but actually it's taking something away. Your intelligence and your concentration, every minute you watch it. That's a true swiz, do you see?

Seated on the floor, Alan shrugs.

I don't want to sound like a spoilsport, old chum – but there really is no substitute for reading. What's the matter: don't you like it?

ALAN: It's all right.

FRANK: I know you think it's none of my beeswax, but it really is you know . . . Actually, it's a disgrace when you come to think of it. You the son of a printer, and never opening a book! If all the world was like you, I'd be out of a job, if you receive my meaning!

DORA: All the same, times change, Frank.

FRANK [reasonably] They change if you let them change, Dora. Please return that set in the morning.

ALAN: [crying out] No!

DORA: Frank! No!

FRANK: I'm sorry, Dora, but I'm not having that thing in the house a moment longer. I told you I didn't want it to begin with.

DORA: But, dear, everyone watches television these days!

FRANK: Yes, and what do they watch? Mindless violence! Mindless jokes! Every five minutes some laughing idiot selling you something you don't want, just to bolster up the economic system. [to Alan] I'm sorry, old chum.

He leaves the scene and sits again in his place.

HESTHER: He's a Communist, then?

DYSART: Old-type Socialist, I'd say. Relentlessly self-improving.

HESTHER: They're *both* older than you'd expect.

DYSART: So I gather.

DORA: [looking after Frank] Really, dear, you are very extreme!

27

She leaves the scene too, and again sits beside her husband.

HESTHER: She's an ex-school teacher, isn't she?

DYSART: Yes. The boy's proud of that. We got on to it this afternoon.

ALAN: [*belligerently, standing up*] She knows more than you.

Hesther crosses and sits by Dysart. During the following, the boy walks round the circle, speaking to Dysart but not looking at him. Dysart replies in the same manner.

DYSART: [*to Alan*] Does she?

ALAN: I bet I do too. I bet I know more history than you.

DYSART: [*to Alan*] Well, I bet you don't.

ALAN: All right: who was the Hammer of the Scots?

DYSART: [*to Alan*] I don't know: who?

ALAN: King Edward the First. Who never smiled again?

DYSART: [*to Alan*] I don't know: who?

ALAN: You don't know anything, do you? It was Henry the First. I know all the Kings.

DYSART: [*to Alan*] And who's your favourite?

ALAN: John.

DYSART: [*to Alan*] Why?

ALAN: Because he put out the eyes of that smarty little –

Pause.

[*sensing he has said something wrong*] Well, he didn't really. He was prevented, because the gaoler was merciful!

HESTHER: Oh dear.

ALAN: *He was prevented!*

DYSART: Something odder was to follow.

ALAN: Who said 'Religion is the opium of the people'?

HESTHER: Good Lord!

Alan giggles.

DYSART: The odd thing was, he said it with a sort of guilty snigger. The sentence is obviously associated with some kind of tension.

HESTHER: What did you say?

DYSART: I gave him the right answer. [*to Alan*] Karl Marx.

ALAN: No.

DYSART: [*to Alan*] Then who?

ALAN: Mind your own beeswax.

28

DYSART: It's probably his dad. He may say it to provoke his wife.

HESTHER: And you mean she's religious?

DYSART: She could be. I tried to discover – none too successfully.

ALAN: Mind your own beeswax!

Alan goes back to bed and lies down in the dark.

DYSART: However, I shall find out on Sunday.

HESTHER: What do you mean?

DYSART: [*getting up*] I want to have a look at his home, so I invited myself over.

HESTHER: Did you?

DYSART: If there's any tension over religion, it should be evident on a Sabbath evening! I'll let you know.

He kisses her cheek and they part, both leaving the square.

Hesther sits in her place again; Dysart walks round the circle, and greets Dora who stands waiting for him downstage.

7.

DYSART: [*shaking hands*] Mrs Strang.

DORA: Mr Strang's still at the Press, I'm afraid. He should be home in a minute.

DYSART: He works Sundays as well?

DORA: Oh, yes. He doesn't set much store by Sundays.

DYSART: Perhaps you and I could have a little talk before he comes in.

DORA: Certainly. Won't you come into the living room?

She leads the way into the square. She is very nervous.

Please....

She motions him to sit, then holds her hands tightly together.

DYSART: Mrs Strang, have you any idea how this thing could have occurred?

DORA: I can't imagine, Doctor. It's all so unbelievable! ...

29

Alan's always been such a gentle boy. He loves animals! Especially horses.

DYSART: Especially?

DORA: Yes. He even has a photograph of one up in his bedroom. A beautiful white one, looking over a gate. His father gave it to him a few years ago, off a calendar he'd printed – and he's never taken it down . . . And when he was seven or eight, I used to have to read him the same book over and over, all *about* a horse.

DYSART: Really?

DORA: Yes: it was called Prince, and no one could ride him.

Alan calls from his bed, not looking at his mother.

ALAN: [*excited, younger voice*] Why not? . . . Why not? . . . Say it! In his voice!

DORA: He loved the idea of animals talking.

DYSART: Did he?

ALAN: *Say it! Say it! . . . Use his voice!*

DORA: [*'proud' voice*] 'Because I am faithful!'

Alan giggles.

'My name is Prince, and I'm a Prince among horses! Only my young Master can ride me! Anyone else – I'll *throw off!*'

Alan giggles louder.

And then I remember I used to tell him a funny thing about falling off horses. Did you know that when Christian cavalry first appeared in the New World, the pagans thought horse and rider was one person?

DYSART: Really?

ALAN: [*sitting up, amazed*] One person?

DORA: Actually, they thought it must be a god.

ALAN: *A god!*

DORA: It was only when one rider fell off, they realized the truth.

DYSART: That's fascinating. I never heard that before. . . . Can you remember anything else like that you may have told him about horses?

DORA: Well, not really. They're in the Bible, of course. 'He saith among the trumpets, Ha, ha.'

DYSART: Ha, ha?

DORA: The Book of Job. Such a noble passage. *You* know –
[*quoting*] 'Hast thou given the horse strength?'
ALAN: [*responding*] 'Hast thou clothed his neck with thunder?'
DORA: [*to Alan*] 'The glory of his nostrils is terrible!'
ALAN: 'He swallows the ground with fierceness and rage!'
DORA: 'He saith among the trumpets —'
ALAN: [*trumpeting*] 'Ha! Ha!'
DORA: [*to Dysart*] Isn't that splendid?
DYSART: It certainly is.
ALAN: [*trumpeting*] Ha! Ha!
DORA: And then, of course, we saw an awful lot of Westerns
on the television. He couldn't have enough of those.
DYSART: But surely you don't have a set, do you? I under-
stood Mr Strang doesn't approve.
DORA: [*conspiratorially*] He doesn't . . . I used to let him slip
off in the afternoons to a friend next door.
DYSART: [*smiling*] You mean without his father's knowledge?
DORA: What the eye does not see, the heart does not grieve
over, does it? Anyway, Westerns are harmless enough,
surely?
Frank stands up and enters the square.
Alan lies back under the blanket.
[*to Frank*] Oh, hallo dear. This is Dr Dysart.
FRANK: [*shaking hands*] How d'you do?
DYSART: How d'you do?
DORA: I was just telling the Doctor, Alan's always adored
horses.
FRANK: [*tight*] We assumed he did.
DORA: You know he did, dear. Look how he liked that photo-
graph you gave him.
FRANK: [*startled*] What about it?
DORA: Nothing dear. Just that he pestered you to have it as
soon as he saw it. Do you remember? [*to Dysart*] We've
always been a horsey family. At least my side of it has. My
grandfather used to ride every morning on the downs behind
Brighton, all dressed up in bowler hat and jodhpurs! He
used to look splendid. Indulging in equitation, he called it.
Frank moves away from them and sits wearily.

ALAN: [*trying the word*] Equitation. . . .

DORA: I remember I told him how that came from *equus*, the Latin word for horse. Alan was fascinated by that word, I know. I suppose because he'd never come across one with two U's together before.

ALAN: [*savouring it*] *Equus!*

DORA: I always wanted the boy to ride himself. He'd have so enjoyed it.

DYSART: But surely he did?

DORA: No.

DYSART: Never?

DORA: He didn't care for it. He was most definite about not wanting to.

DYSART: But he must have had to at the stables? I mean, it would be part of the job.

DORA: You'd have thought so, but no. He absolutely wouldn't, would he, dear?

FRANK: [*dryly*] It seems he was perfectly happy raking out manure.

DYSART: Did he ever give a reason for this?

DORA: No. I must say we both thought it most peculiar, but he wouldn't discuss it. I mean, you'd have thought he'd be longing to get out in the air after being cooped up all week in that dreadful shop. Electrical and kitchenware! Isn't *that* an environment for a sensitive boy, Doctor? . . .

FRANK: Dear, have you offered the doctor a cup of tea?

DORA: Oh dear, no, I haven't! . . . And you must be dying for one.

DYSART: That would be nice.

DORA: Of course it would . . . Excuse me . . .

She goes out – but lingers on the circle, eavesdropping near the right door. Alan stretches out under his blanket and sleeps. Frank gets up.

FRANK: My wife has romantic ideas, if you receive my meaning.

DYSART: About her family?

FRANK: She thinks she married beneath her. I daresay she did. I don't understand these things myself.

32

DYSART: Mr Strang, I'm fascinated by the fact that Alan wouldn't ride.

FRANK: Yes, well that's him. He's always been a weird lad, I have to be honest. Can you imagine spending your weekends like that – just cleaning out stalls – with all the things that he could have been doing in the way of Further Education?

DYSART: Except he's hardly a scholar.

FRANK: How do we know? He's never really tried. His mother indulged him. She doesn't care if he can hardly write his own name, and she a school teacher that was. Just as long as he's happy, she says . . .

Dora wrings her hands in anguish.

Frank sits again.

DYSART: Would you say she was closer to him than you are?

FRANK: They've always been thick as thieves. I can't say I entirely approve – especially when I hear her whispering that Bible to him hour after hour, up there in his room.

DYSART: Your wife is religious?

FRANK: Some might say excessively so. Mind you, that's her business. But when it comes to dosing it down the boy's throat – well, frankly, he's my son as well as hers. She doesn't see that. Of course, that's the funny thing about religious people. They always think their susceptibilities are more important than non-religious.

DYSART: And you're non-religious, I take it?

FRANK: I'm an atheist, and I don't mind admitting it. If you want my opinion, it's the Bible that's responsible for all this.

DYSART: Why?

FRANK: Well, look at it yourself. A boy spends night after night having this stuff read into him: an innocent man tortured to death – thorns driven into his head – nails into his hands – a spear jammed through his ribs. It can mark anyone for life, that kind of thing. I'm not joking. The boy was absolutely fascinated by all that. He was always mooning over religious pictures. I mean real kinky ones, if you receive my meaning. I had to put a stop to it once or twice! . . . [*pause*] Bloody religion – it's our only real problem in this house, but it's insuperable: I don't mind admitting it.

33

Unable to stand any more, Dora comes in again.

DORA: [*pleasantly*] You must excuse my husband, Doctor. This one subject is something of an obsession with him, isn't it, dear? You must admit.

FRANK: Call it what you like. All that stuff to me is just bad sex.

DORA: And what has that got to do with Alan?

FRANK: Everything!... [*seriously*] Everything, Dora!

DORA: I don't understand. What are you saying?

He turns away from her.

DYSART: [*calmingly*] Mr Strang, exactly how informed do you judge your son to *be* about sex?

FRANK: [*tight*] I don't know.

DYSART: You didn't actually instruct him yourself?

FRANK: Not in so many words, no.

DYSART: Did *you*, Mrs Strang?

DORA: Well, I spoke a little, yes. I had to. I've been a teacher, Doctor, and I know what happens if you don't. They find out through magazines and dirty books.

DYSART: What sort of thing did you tell him? I'm sorry if this is embarrassing.

DORA: I told him the biological facts. But I also told him what I believed. That sex is not *just* a biological matter, but spiritual as well. That if God willed, he would fall in love one day. That his task was to prepare himself for the most important happening of his life. And after that, if he was lucky, he might come to know a higher love still . . . I simply . . . don't understand. . . . *Alan!* . . .

She breaks down in sobs.

Her husband gets up and goes to her.

FRANK: [*embarrassed*] There now. There now, Dora. Come on!

DORA: [*with sudden desperation*] All right – laugh! Laugh, as usual!

FRANK: [*kindly*] No one's laughing, Dora.

She glares at him. He puts his arms round her shoulders.

No one's laughing, are they Doctor?

Tenderly, he leads his wife out of the square, and they resume their places on the bench.

Lights grow much dimmer.

34

8.

A strange noise begins. Alan begins to murmur from his bed. He is having a bad nightmare, moving his hands and body as if frantically straining to tug something back. Dysart leaves the square as the boy's cries increase.

ALAN: Ek!... Ek!... *Ek!...*

Cries of Ek! *on tape fill the theatre, from all around. Dysart reaches the foot of Alan's bed as the boy gives a terrible cry —*

EK!

— and wakes up. The sounds snap off. Alan and the Doctor stare at each other. Then abruptly Dysart leaves the area and re-enters the square.

9.

Lights grow brighter.
Dysart sits on his bench, left, and opens his file. Alan gets out of bed, leaves his blanket, and comes in. He looks truculent.

DYSART: Hallo. How are you this morning?

Alan stares at him.

Come on: sit down.

Alan crosses the stage and sits on the bench, opposite.

Sorry if I gave you a start last night. I was collecting some papers from my office, and I thought I'd look in on you. Do you dream often?

ALAN: Do *you?*

DYSART: It's my job to ask the questions. Yours to answer them.

ALAN: Says who?

DYSART: Says me. Do you dream often?

ALAN: Do you?

DYSART: Look – Alan.

ALAN: I'll answer if you answer. In turns.

Pause.

35

DYSART: Very well. Only we have to speak the truth.
ALAN: [*mocking*] Very well.
DYSART: So. Do you dream often?
ALAN: Yes. Do you?
DYSART: Yes. Do you have a special dream?
ALAN: No. Do you?
DYSART: Yes. What was your dream about last night?
ALAN: Can't remember. What's yours about?
DYSART: I said the truth.
ALAN: That is the truth. What's yours about? The special one.
DYSART: Carving up children.
> *Alan smiles.*

My turn!
ALAN: What?
DYSART: What is your first memory of a horse?
ALAN: What d'you mean?
DYSART: The first time one entered your life, in any way.
ALAN: Can't remember.
DYSART: Are you sure?
ALAN: Yes.
DYSART: You have no recollection of the first time you noticed a horse?
ALAN: I told you. Now it's my turn. Are you married?
DYSART: [*controlling himself*] I am.
ALAN: Is she a doctor too?
DYSART: It's my turn.
ALAN: Yes, well what?
DYSART: What is Ek?
> *Pause.*

You shouted it out last night in your sleep. I thought you might like to talk about it.
ALAN: [*singing*] Double Diamond works wonders,
Works wonders, works wonders!
DYSART: Come on, now. You can do better than that.
ALAN: [*singing louder*] Double Diamond works wonders,
Works wonders
For you!
DYSART: All right. Good morning.

ALAN: What d'you mean?
DYSART: We're finished for today.
ALAN: But I've only had ten minutes.
DYSART: Too bad.
He picks up a file and studies it.
Alan lingers.
Didn't you hear me? I said, Good morning.
ALAN: That's not fair!
DYSART: No?
ALAN: [*savagely*] The Government pays you twenty quid an hour to see me. I know. I heard downstairs.
DYSART: Well, go back there and hear some more.
ALAN: *That's not fair!*
He springs up, clenching his fists in a sudden violent rage.
You're a – you're a – You're a swiz! . . . Bloody swiz! . . . Fucking swiz!
DYSART: Do I have to call Nurse?
ALAN: She puts a finger on me, I'll bash her!
DYSART: She'll bash you much harder, I can assure you. Now go away.
He reads his file. Alan stays where he is, emptily clenching his hands. He turns away.
A pause.
A faint hum starts from the Chorus.
ALAN: [*sullenly*] On a beach. . . .

10.

He steps out of the square, upstage, and begins to walk round the circle. Warm light glows on it.
DYSART: What?
ALAN: Where I saw a horse. Swizzy.
Lazily he kicks at the sand, and throws stones at the sea.
DYSART: How old were you?
ALAN: How should I know? . . . Six.
DYSART: Well, go on. What were you doing there?

37

ALAN: Digging.

He throws himself on the ground, downstage centre of the circle, and starts scuffing with his hands.

DYSART: A sandcastle?

ALAN: Well, what else?

DYSART: [*warningly*] And?

ALAN: Suddenly I heard this noise. Coming up behind me.

A young Horseman issues in slow motion *out of the tunnel. He carries a riding crop with which he is urging on his invisible horse, down the right side of the circle.*

The hum increases.

DYSART: What noise?

ALAN: Hooves. Splashing.

DYSART: Splashing?

ALAN: The tide was out and he was galloping.

DYSART: Who was?

ALAN: This fellow. Like a college chap. He was on a big horse – urging him on. I thought he hadn't seen me. I called out: Hey!

The horseman goes into natural time, *charging fast round the downstage corner of the square straight at Alan.*

and they just swerved in time!

HORSEMAN: [*reining back*] Whoa!... Whoa there! *Whoa!*... Sorry! I didn't see you!... Did I scare you?

ALAN: No!

HORSEMAN: [*looking down on him*] That's a terrific castle!

ALAN: What's his name?

HORSEMAN: Trojan. You can stroke him, if you like. He won't mind.

Shyly Alan stretches up on tip-toe, and pats an invisible shoulder.

[*amused*] You can hardly reach down there. Would you like to come up?

Alan nods, eyes wide.

All right. Come round this side. You always mount a horse from the left. I'll give you a lift. O.K.?

Alan goes round on the other side.

Here we go, now. Just do nothing. Upsadaisy!

Alan set his foot on the Horseman's thigh, and is lifted by him up on to his shoulders.
The hum from the Chorus becomes exultant. Then stops.
All right?
Alan nods.
Good. Now all you do is hold onto his mane.
He holds up the crop, and Alan grips on to it.
Tight now. And grip with your knees. All right?
All set?... Come on, then, Trojan. Let's go!
The Horseman walks slowly upstage round the circle, with Alan's legs tight round his neck.
DYSART: How was it? Was it wonderful?
Alan rides in silence.
Can't you remember?
HORSEMAN: Do you want to go faster?
ALAN: Yes!
HORSEMAN: O.K. All you have to do is say 'Come on, Trojan – bear me away!'... Say it, then!
ALAN: Bear me away!
The Horseman starts to run with Alan round the circle.
DYSART: You went fast?
ALAN: Yes!
DYSART: Weren't you frightened?
ALAN: No!
HORSEMAN: Come on now, Trojan! Bear us away! Hold on! Come on now!...
He runs faster. Alan begins to laugh. Then suddenly, as they reach again the right downstage corner, Frank and Dora stand up in alarm.
DORA: Alan!
FRANK: Alan!
DORA: Alan, stop!
Frank runs round after them. Dora follows behind.
FRANK: Hey, you! You!...
HORSEMAN: Whoa, boy!... Whoa!...
He reins the horse round, and wheels to face the parents. This all goes fast.
FRANK: What do you imagine you are doing?

39

HORSEMAN: [*ironic*] 'Imagine'?

FRANK: What is my son doing up there?

HORSEMAN: Water-skiing!

Dora joins them, breathless.

DORA: Is he all right, Frank?... He's not hurt?

FRANK: Don't you think you should ask permission before doing a stupid thing like that?

HORSEMAN: What's stupid?

ALAN: It's lovely, dad!

DORA: Alan, come down here!

HORSEMAN: The boy's perfectly safe. Please don't be hysterical.

FRANK: Don't you be la-di-da with me, young man! Come down here, Alan. You heard what your mother said.

ALAN: No.

FRANK: Come down at once. Right this moment.

ALAN: No.... NO!

FRANK: [*in a fury*] I said – this moment!

He pulls Alan from the horseman's shoulders. The boy shrieks, and falls to the ground.

HORSEMAN: Watch it!

DORA: Frank!

She runs to her son, and kneels. The horseman skitters.

HORSEMAN: Are you mad? D'you want to terrify the horse?

DORA: He's grazed his knee. Frank – the boy's hurt!

ALAN: I'm not! I'm *not!*

FRANK: What's your name?

HORSEMAN: Jesse James.

DORA: Frank, he's bleeding!

FRANK: I intend to report you to the police for endangering the lives of children.

HORSEMAN: Go right ahead!

DORA: Can you stand, dear?

ALAN: Oh, *stop* it!...

FRANK: You're a public menace, d'you know that? How dare you pick up children and put them on dangerous animals.

HORSEMAN: Dangerous?

FRANK: Of course dangerous. Look at his eyes. They're rolling.

HORSEMAN: So are yours!

FRANK: In my opinion that is a dangerous animal. In my considered opinion you are both dangers to the safety of this beach.

HORSEMAN: And in my opinion, you're a stupid fart!

DORA: Frank, leave it!

FRANK: What did you say?

DORA: It's not important, Frank – really!

FRANK: *What did you say?*

HORSEMAN: Oh bugger off! Sorry, chum! Come on, Trojan!

He urges his horse straight at them, then wheels it and gallops off round the right side of the circle and away up the tunnel, out of sight. The parents cry out, as they are covered with sand and water. Frank runs after him, and round the left side of the circle, with his wife following after.

ALAN: Splash, splash, splash! All three of us got covered with water! Dad got absolutely soaked!

FRANK: [*shouting after the Horseman*] Hooligan! Filthy hooligan!

ALAN: I wanted to laugh!

FRANK: Upper class riff-raff! That's all they are, people who go riding! That's what they *want* – trample on ordinary people!

DORA: Don't be absurd, Frank.

FRANK: It's why they do it. It's why they bloody do it!

DORA: [*amused*] Look at you. You're covered!

FRANK: Not as much as you. There's sand all over your hair!

She starts to laugh.

[*shouting*] Hooligan! Bloody hooligan!

She starts to laugh more. He tries to brush the sand out of her hair.

What are you laughing at? It's not funny. It's not funny at all, Dora!

She goes off, right, still laughing. Alan edges into the square, still on the ground.

It's just not funny! ...

Frank returns to his place on the beach, sulky.

Abrupt silence.
ALAN: And that's all I remember.
DYSART: And a lot, too. Thank you . . . You know, I've never been on a horse in my life.
ALAN: [*not looking at him*] Nor me.
DYSART: You mean, after that?
ALAN: Yes.
DYSART: But you must have done at the stables?
ALAN: No.
DYSART: Never?
ALAN: No.
DYSART: How come?
ALAN: I didn't care to.
DYSART: Did it have anything to do with falling off like that, all those years ago?
ALAN: [*tight*] I just didn't care to, that's all.
DYSART: Do you think of that scene often?
ALAN: I suppose.
DYSART: Why, do you think?
ALAN: 'Cos it's funny.
DYSART: Is that all?
ALAN: What else? My turn. . . . I told you a secret: now you tell me one.
DYSART: All right. I have patients who've got things to tell me, only they're ashamed to say them to my face. What do you think I do about that?
ALAN: What?
DYSART: I give them this little tape recorder.
He takes a small tape recorder and microphone from his pocket.
They go off to another room, and send me the tape through Nurse. They don't have to listen to it with me.
ALAN: That's stupid.
DYSART: All you do is press this button, and speak into this. It's very simple. Anyway, your time's up for today. I'll see you tomorrow.
ALAN: [*getting up*] Maybe.
DYSART: Maybe?

ALAN: If I feel like it.
He is about to go out. Then suddenly he returns to Dysart and takes the machine from him.
It's stupid.
He leaves the square and goes back to his bed.

II.

DORA: [*calling out*] Doctor!
Dora re-enters and comes straight on to the square from the right. She wears an overcoat, and is nervously carrying a shopping bag.
DYSART: That same evening, his mother appeared.
DORA: Hallo, Doctor.
DYSART: Mrs Strang!
DORA: I've been shopping in the neighbourhood. I thought I might just look in.
DYSART: Did you want to see Alan?
DORA: [*uncomfortably*] No, no . . . Not just at the moment. Actually, it's more you I wanted to see.
DYSART: Yes?
DORA: You see, there's something Mr Strang and I thought you ought to know. We discussed it, and it might just be important.
DYSART: Well, come and sit down.
DORA: I can't stay more than a moment. I'm late as it is. Mr Strang will be wanting his dinner.
DYSART: Ah. [*encouragingly*] So, what was it you wanted to tell me?
She sits on the upstage bench.
DORA: Well, do you remember that photograph I mentioned to you. The one Mr Strang gave Alan to decorate his bedroom a few years ago?
DYSART: Yes. A horse looking over a gate, wasn't it?
DORA: That's right. Well, actually, it took the place of another kind of picture altogether.
DYSART: What kind?

43

DORA: It was a reproduction of Our Lord on his way to Calvary. Alan found it in Reeds Art Shop, and fell absolutely in love with it. He insisted on buying it with his pocket money, and hanging it at the foot of his bed where he could see it last thing at night. My husband was very displeased.

DYSART: Because it was religious?

DORA: In all fairness I must admit it was a little extreme. The Christ was loaded down with chains, and the centurions were really laying on the stripes. It certainly would not have been my choice, but I don't believe in interfering too much with children, so I said nothing.

DYSART: But Mr Strang did?

DORA: He stood it for a while, but one day we had one of our tiffs about religion, and he went straight upstairs, tore it off the boy's wall and threw it in the dustbin. Alan went quite hysterical. He cried for days without stopping – and he was not a crier, you know.

DYSART: But he recovered when he was given the photograph of the horse in its place?

DORA: He certainly seemed to. At least, he hung it in exactly the same position, and we had no more of that awful weeping.

DYSART: Thank you, Mrs Strang. That *is* interesting . . . Exactly how long ago was that? Can you remember?

DORA: It must be five years ago, Doctor. Alan would have been about twelve. How is he, by the way?

DYSART: Bearing up.

She rises.

DORA: Please give him my love.

DYSART: You can see him any time you want, you know.

DORA: Perhaps if I could come one afternoon without Mr Strang. He and Alan don't exactly get on at the moment, as you can imagine.

DYSART: Whatever you decide, Mrs Strang . . . Oh, one thing.

DORA: Yes?

DYSART: Could you describe that photograph of the horse in a little more detail for me? I presume it's still in his bedroom?

DORA: Oh, yes. It's a most remarkable picture, really. You

very rarely see a horse taken from that angle – absolutely head on. That's what makes it so interesting.

DYSART: Why? What does it look like?

DORA: Well, it's most extraordinary. It comes out all eyes.

DYSART: Staring straight at you?

DORA: Yes, that's right . . .

An uncomfortable pause.

I'll come and see him one day very soon, Doctor. Goodbye.

She leaves, and resumes her place by her husband.

DYSART: [*to audience*] It was then – that moment – I felt real alarm. What was it? The shadow of a giant head across my desk? . . . At any rate, the feeling got worse with the stable-owner's visit.

12.

Dalton comes in to the square: heavy-set: mid-fifties.

DALTON: Dr Dysart?

DYSART: Mr Dalton. It's very good of you to come.

DALTON: It is, actually. In my opinion the boy should be in prison. Not in a hospital at the tax-payers' expense.

DYSART: Please sit down.

Dalton sits.

This must have been a terrible experience for you.

DALTON: Terrible? I don't think I'll ever get over it. Jill's had a nervous breakdown.

DYSART: Jill?

DALTON: The girl who worked for me. Of course, she feels responsible in a way. Being the one who introduced him in the first place.

DYSART: He was introduced to the stable by a girl?

DALTON: Jill Mason. He met her somewhere, and asked for a job. She told him to come and see me. I wish to Christ she never had.

DYSART: But when he first appeared he didn't seem in any way peculiar?

45

DALTON: No, he was bloody good. He'd spend hours with the horses cleaning and grooming them, way over the call of duty. I thought he was a real find.

DYSART: Apparently, during the whole time he worked for you, he never actually rode.

DALTON: That's true.

DYSART: Wasn't that peculiar?

DALTON: Very... *If* he didn't.

DYSART: What do you mean?

Dalton rises.

DALTON: Because on and off, that whole year, I had the feeling the horses were being taken out at night.

DYSART: At night?

DALTON: There were just odd things I noticed. I mean too often one or other of them would be sweaty first thing in the morning, when it wasn't sick. Very sweaty, too. And its stall wouldn't be near as mucky as it should be if it had been in all night. I never paid it much mind at the time. It was only when I realised I'd been hiring a loony, I came to wonder if he hadn't been riding all the time, behind our backs.

DYSART: But wouldn't you have noticed if things had been disturbed?

DALTON: Nothing ever was. Still, he's a neat worker. That wouldn't prove anything.

DYSART: Aren't the stables locked at night?

DALTON: Yes.

DYSART: And someone sleeps on the premises?

DALTON: Me and my son.

DYSART: Two people?

DALTON: I'm sorry, Doctor. It's obviously just my fancy. I tell you, this thing has shaken me so bad, I'm liable to believe anything. If there's nothing else, I'll be going.

DYSART: Look: even if you were right, why should anyone do that? Why would any boy prefer to ride by himself at night, when he could go off with others during the day.

DALTON: Are you asking me? He's a loony, isn't he?

Dalton leaves the square and sits again in his place. Dysart watches him go.

ALAN: It was *sexy*.
DYSART: His tape arrived that evening.

13.

Alan is sitting on his bed holding the tape-recorder. Nurse approaches briskly, takes the machine from him – gives it to Dysart in the square – and leaves again, resuming her seat. Dysart switches on the tape.
ALAN: That's what you want to know, isn't it? All right: it was. I'm talking about the beach. That time when I was a kid. What I told you about. . . .
Pause. He is in great emotional difficulty.
Dysart sits on the left bench listening, file in hand. Alan rises and stands directly behind him, but on the circle, as if recording the ensuing speech. He never, of course, looks directly at the Doctor.
I was pushed forward on the horse. There was sweat on my legs from his neck. The fellow held me tight, and let me turn the horse which way I wanted. All that power going any way you wanted . . . His sides were all warm, and the smell . . . Then suddenly I was on the ground, where Dad pulled me. I could have bashed him . . .
Pause.
Something else. When the horse first appeared, I looked up into his mouth. It was huge. There was this chain in it. The fellow pulled it, and cream dripped out. I said 'Does it hurt?' And he said – the horse said – said –
He stops, in anguish. Dysart makes a note in his file.
[*desperately*] It was always the same, after that. Every time I heard one clop by, I had to run and see. Up a country lane or anywhere. They sort of pulled me. I couldn't take my eyes off them. Just to watch their skins. The way their necks twist, and sweat shines in the folds . . . [*pause*] I can't remember when it started. Mum reading to me about Prince who no one could ride, except one boy. Or the white horse in Revelations. 'He that sat upon him was called Faithful and True. His eyes

were as flames of fire, and he had a name written that no man knew but himself' . . . Words like reins. Stirrup. Flanks . . . 'Dashing his spurs against his charger's flanks!' . . . Even the words made me feel – . . . Years, I never told anyone. Mum wouldn't understand. She likes 'Equitation'. Bowler hats and jodhpurs! 'My grandfather dressed for the horse,' she says. What does that mean? The horse isn't dressed. It's the most naked thing you ever saw! More than a dog or a cat or anything. Even the most broken down old nag has got its *life!* To put a bowler on it is *filthy!* . . . Putting them through their paces! Bloody gymkhanas! . . . No one understands! . . . Except cowboys. They do. I wish I was a cowboy. They're free. They just swing up and then it's miles of grass . . . I bet all cowboys are *orphans!* . . . I bet they are!

NURSE: Mr Strang to see you, Doctor.

DYSART: [*in surprise*] Mr Strang? Show him up, please.

ALAN: No one ever says to cowboys 'Receive my meaning'! They wouldn't dare. Or 'God' all the time. [*mimicking his mother*] 'God sees you, Alan. God's got eyes everywhere—'

He stops abruptly.

I'm not doing any more! . . . I hate this! . . . You can whistle for anymore. I've had it!

He returns angrily to his bed, throwing the blanket over him.

Dysart switches off the tape.

14.

Frank Strang comes into the square, his hat in his hand. He is nervous and embarrassed.

DYSART: [*welcoming*] Hallo, Mr Strang.

FRANK: I was just passing. I hope it's not too late.

DYSART: Of course not. I'm delighted to see you.

FRANK: My wife doesn't know I'm here. I'd be grateful to you if you didn't enlighten her, if you receive my meaning.

DYSART: Everything that happens in this room is confidential, Mr Strang.

FRANK: I hope so ... I hope so ...

DYSART: [*gently*] Do you have something to tell me?

FRANK: As a matter of fact I have. Yes.

DYSART: Your wife told me about the photograph.

FRANK: I know, it's not that! It's *about* that, but it's – worse.
... I wanted to tell you the other night, but I couldn't in
front of Dora. Maybe I should have. It might show her
where all that stuff leads to, she drills into the boy behind
my back.

DYSART: What kind of thing is it?

FRANK: Something I witnessed.

DYSART: Where?

FRANK: At home. About eighteen months ago.

DYSART: Go on.

FRANK: It was late. I'd gone upstairs to fetch something. The
boy had been in bed hours, or so I thought.

DYSART: Go on.

FRANK: As I came along the passage I saw the door of his bedroom was ajar. I'm sure he didn't know it was. From inside I
heard the sound of this chanting.

DYSART: Chanting?

FRANK: Like the Bible. One of those lists his mother's always
reading to him.

DYSART: What kind of list?

FRANK: Those Begats. So-and-so begat, you know. Genealogy.

DYSART: Can you remember what Alan's list sounded like?

FRANK: Well, the *sort* of thing. I stood there absolutely
astonished. The first word I heard was ...

ALAN: [*rising and chanting*] Prince!

DYSART: Prince?

FRANK: Prince begat Prance. That sort of nonsense.

Alan moves slowly to the centre of the circle, downstage.

ALAN: And Prance begat Prankus! And Prankus begat
Flankus!

FRANK: I looked through the door, and he was standing in the
moonlight in his pyjamas, right in front of that big photograph.

DYSART: The horse with the huge eyes?

FRANK: Right.

49

ALAN: Flankus begat Spankus. And Spankus begat Spunkus the Great, who lived three score years!

FRANK: It was all like that. I can't remember the exact names, of course. Then suddenly he knelt down.

DYSART: In front of the photograph?

FRANK: Yes. Right there at the foot of his bed.

ALAN: [*kneeling*] And Legwus begat Neckwus. And Neckwus begat Fleckwus, the King of Spit. And Fleckwus spoke out of his chinkle-chankle!

He bows himself to the ground.

DYSART: What?

FRANK: I'm sure that was the word. I've never forgotten it. Chinkle-chankle.

Alan raises his head and extends his hands up in glory.

ALAN: And he said 'Behold – I give you Equus, my only begotten son!'

DYSART: Equus?

FRANK: Yes. No doubt of that. He repeated that word several times. 'Equus my only begotten son.'

ALAN: [*reverently*] Ek . . . . wus!

DYSART: [*suddenly understanding: almost 'aside'*] Ek . . . . Ek . . . .

FRANK: [*embarrassed*] And then . . .

DYSART: Yes: what?

FRANK: He took a piece of string out of his pocket. Made up into a noose. And put it in his mouth.

Alan bridles himself with invisible string, and pulls it back.

And then with his other hand he picked up a coat hanger. A wooden coat hanger, and – and—

DYSART: Began to beat himself?

Alan, in mime, begins to thrash himself, increasing the strokes in speed and viciousness.

Pause.

FRANK: You see why I couldn't tell his mother. . . . Religion. Religion's at the bottom of all this!

DYSART: What did you do?

FRANK: Nothing. I coughed – and went back downstairs.

The boy starts guiltily – tears the string from his mouth – and scrambles back to bed.

DYSART: Did you ever speak to him about it later? Even obliquely?
FRANK: [*unhappily*] I can't speak of things like that, Doctor. It's not in my nature.
DYSART: [*kindly*] No. I see that.
FRANK: But I thought you ought to know. So I came.
DYSART: [*warmly*] Yes. I'm very grateful to you. Thank you.
   Pause.
FRANK: Well, that's it . . .
DYSART: Is there anything else?
FRANK: [*even more embarrassed*] There is actually. One thing.
DYSART: What's that?
FRANK: On the night that he did it – that awful thing in the stable –
DYSART: Yes?
FRANK: That very night, he was out with a girl.
DYSART: How d'you know that?
FRANK: I just know.
DYSART: [*puzzled*] Did he tell you?
FRANK: I can't say any more.
DYSART: I don't quite understand.
FRANK: Everything said in here is confidential, you said.
DYSART: Absolutely.
FRANK: Then ask him. Ask him about taking a girl out, that very night he did it. . . . [*abruptly*] Goodbye, Doctor.
   He goes. Dysart looks after him.
   Frank resumes his seat.

15.

   Alan gets up and enters the square.
DYSART: Alan! Come in. Sit down. [*pleasantly*] What did you do last night?
ALAN: Watched telly.
DYSART: Any good?
ALAN: All right.
DYSART: Thanks for the tape. It was excellent.

51

ALAN: I'm not making any more.

DYSART: One thing I didn't quite understand. You began to say something about the horse on the beach talking to you.

ALAN: That's stupid. Horses don't talk.

DYSART: So I believe.

ALAN: I don't know what you mean.

DYSART: Never mind. Tell me something else. Who introduced you to the stable to begin with?

Pause.

ALAN: Someone I met.

DYSART: Where?

ALAN: Bryson's.

DYSART: The shop where you worked?

ALAN: Yes.

DYSART: That's a funny place for you to be. Whose idea was that?

ALAN: Dad.

DYSART: I'd have thought he'd have wanted you to work with him.

ALAN: I haven't the aptitude. And printing's a failing trade. If you receive my meaning.

DYSART: [*amused*] I see . . . What did your mother think?

ALAN: Shops are common.

DYSART: And you?

ALAN: I loved it.

DYSART: Really?

ALAN: [*sarcastic*] Why not? You get to spend every minute with electrical things. It's fun.

Nurse, Dalton and the actors playing horses call out to him as Customers, seated where they are. Their voices are aggressive and demanding. There is a constant background mumbling, made up of trade names, out of which can clearly be distinguished the italicized words, which are shouted out.

CUSTOMER: *Philco!*

ALAN: [*to Dysart*] Of course it might just drive you off your chump.

CUSTOMER: I want to buy a hot-plate. I'm told the *Philco* is a good make!
ALAN: I think it is, madam.
CUSTOMER: *Remington* ladies' shavers?
ALAN: I'm not sure, madam.
CUSTOMER: *Robex* tableware?
CUSTOMER: *Croydex?*
CUSTOMER: *Volex?*
CUSTOMER: *Pifco* automatic toothbrushes?
ALAN: I'll find out, sir.
CUSTOMER: Beautiflor!
CUSTOMER: Windowlene!
CUSTOMER: I want a *Philco* transistor radio!
CUSTOMER: This isn't a *Remington!* I wanted a *Remington!*
ALAN: Sorry.
CUSTOMER: Are you a dealer for *Hoover?*
ALAN: Sorry.
CUSTOMER: I wanted the heat retaining *Pifco!*
ALAN: *Sorry!*
    Jill comes into the square: a girl in her early twenties, pretty and middle class. She wears a sweater and jeans. The mumbling stops.
JILL Hallo.
ALAN: Hallo.
JILL: Have you any blades for a clipping machine?
JILL: Clipping?
JILL: To clip horses.
    Pause. He stares at her, open-mouthed.
    What's the matter?
ALAN: You work at Dalton's stables. I've seen you.
    During the following, he mimes putting away a pile of boxes on a shelf in the shop.
JILL: I've seen you too, haven't I? You're the boy who's always staring into the yard around lunch-time.
ALAN: Me?
JILL: You're there most days.
ALAN: Not me.
JILL: [*amused*] Of course it's you. Mr Dalton was only saying

53

the other day: 'Who's that boy keeps staring in at the door?'
Are you looking for a job or something?
ALAN: [*eagerly*] Is there one?
JILL: I don't know.
ALAN: I can only do weekends.
JILL: That's when most people ride. We can always use extra
hands. It'd mainly be mucking out.
ALAN: I don't mind.
JILL: Can you ride?
ALAN: No ... No ... I don't want to.
She looks at him curiously.
Please.
JILL: Come up on Saturday. I'll introduce you to Mr Dalton.
She leaves the square.
DYSART: When was this? About a year ago?
ALAN: I suppose.
DYSART: And she did?
ALAN: Yes.
*Briskly he moves the three benches to form three stalls in
the stable.*

16.

Rich light falls on the square.
An exultant humming from the Chorus.
*Tramping is heard. Three actors playing horses rise from
their places. Together they unhook three horse masks from
the ladders to left and right, put them on with rigid
timing, and walk with swaying horse-motion into the
square. Their metal hooves stamp on the wood. Their
masks turn and toss high above their heads – as they will
do sporadically throughout all horse scenes – making the
steel gleam in the light.*
*For a moment they seem to converge on the boy as he
stands in the middle of the stable, but then they swiftly
turn and take up positions as if tethered by the head, with
their invisible rumps towards him, one by each bench.*

*Alan is sunk in this glowing world of horses. Lost in
wonder, he starts almost involuntarily to kneel on the
floor in reverence – but is sharply interrupted by the
cheery voice of Dalton, coming into the stable, followed by
Jill. The boy straightens up guiltily.*

DALTON: First thing to learn is drill. Learn it and keep to it. I
want this place neat, dry and clean at all times. After you've
mucked out, Jill will show you some grooming. What we call
strapping a horse.

JILL: I think Trooper's got a stone.

DALTON: Yes? Let's see.

*He crosses to the horse by the left bench, who is balancing
one hoof on its tip. He picks up the hoof.*

You're right. [*to Alan*] See this? This V here. It's what's
called a frog. Sort of shock-absorber. Once you pierce that, it
takes ages to heal – so you want to watch for it. You clean it
out with this. What we call a hoof-pick.

He takes from his pocket an invisible pick.

Mind how you go with it. It's very sharp. Use it like this.

He quickly takes the stone out.

See?

Alan nods, fascinated.

You'll soon get the hang of it. Jill will look after you. What
she doesn't know about stables, isn't worth knowing.

JILL: [*pleased*] Oh yes, I'm sure!

DALTON: [*handing Alan the pick*] Careful how you go with
that. The main rule is, anything you don't know: ask. Never
pretend you know something when you don't. [*smiling*]
Actually, the main rule is: enjoy yourself. All right?

ALAN: Yes, sir.

DALTON: Good lad. See you later.

*He nods to them cheerfully, and leaves the square. Alan
clearly puts the invisible hoof-pick on the rail, downstage
left.*

JILL: All right, let's start on some grooming. Why don't we
begin with him? He looks as if he needs it.

*They approach Nugget, who is standing to the right. She
pats him. Alan sits and watches her.*

55

This is Nugget. He's my favourite. He's as gentle as a baby, aren't you? But terribly fast if you want him to be.

During the following, she mimes both the actions and the objects, which she picks up from the right bench.

Now this is the dandy, and we start with that. Then you move on to the body brush. This is the most important, and you use it with this curry-comb. Now you always groom the same way: from the ears downward. Don't be afraid to do it hard. The harder you do it, the more the horse loves it. Push it right through the coat: like this.

The boy watches in fascination as she brushes the invisible body of Nugget, scraping the dirt and hair off on to the invisible curry-comb. Now and then the horse mask moves very slightly in pleasure.

Down towards the tail and right through the coat. See how he loves it? I'm giving you a lovely massage, boy, aren't I? ... You try.

She hands him the brush. Gingerly he rises and approaches Nugget. Embarrassed and excited, he copies her movements, inexpertly.

Keep it nice and easy. Never rush. Down towards the tail and right through the coat. That's it. Again. Down towards the tail and right through the coat. . . . Very good. Now you keep that up for fifteen minutes and then do old Trooper. Will you?

Alan nods.

You've got a feel for it. I can tell. It's going to be nice teaching you. See you later.

She leaves the square and resumes her place.

Alan is left alone with the horses.

They all stamp. He approaches Nugget again, and touches the horse's shoulder. The mask turns sharply in his direction. The boy pauses, then moves his hand gently over the outline of the neck and back. The mask is re-assured. It stares ahead unmoving. Then Alan lifts his palm to his face and smells it deeply, closing his eyes.

Dysart rises from his bench, and begins to walk slowly upstage round the circle.

56

DYSART: Was that good? Touching them.

Alan gives a faint groan.

ALAN: Mmm.

DYSART: It must have been marvellous, being near them at last . . . Stroking them . . . Making them fresh and glossy . . . Tell me . . .

Silence. Alan begins to brush Nugget.

How about the girl? Did you like her?

ALAN: [*tight*] All right.

DYSART: Just all right?

Alan changes his position, moving round Nugget's rump so that his back is to the audience. He brushes harder. Dysart comes downstage around the circle, and finally back to his bench.

Was she friendly?

ALAN: Yes.

DYSART: Or stand-offish?

ALAN: Yes.

DYSART: Well which?

ALAN: What?

DYSART: Which was she?

Alan brushes harder.

Did you take her out? Come on now: tell me. Did you have a date with her?

ALAN: What?

DYSART: [*sitting*] Tell me if you did.

The boy suddenly explodes in one of his rages.

ALAN: [*yelling*] TELL ME!

All the masks toss at the noise.

DYSART: What?

ALAN: *Tell me, tell me, tell me, tell me!*

Alan storms out of the square, and downstage to where Dysart sits. He is raging. During the ensuing, the horses leave by all three openings.

On and on, sitting there! Nosey Parker! That's all you are! Bloody Nosey Parker! Just like Dad. On and on and bloody on! Tell me, tell me, tell me! . . . Answer this. Answer that. Never stop! –

He marches round the circle and back into the square.
Dysart rises and enters it from the other side.

17.

Lights brighten.
DYSART: I'm sorry.
Alan slams about what is now the office again, replacing the benches to their usual position.
ALAN: All right, it's my turn now. You tell me! Answer me!
DYSART: We're not playing that game now.
ALAN: We're playing what I say.
DYSART: All right. What do you want to know?
He sits.
ALAN: Do *you* have dates?
DYSART: I told you. I'm married.
Alan approaches him, very hostile.
ALAN: I know. Her name's Margaret. She's a dentist! You see, I found out! What made you go with her? Did you use to bite her hands when she did you in the chair?
The boy sits next to him, close.
DYSART: That's not very funny.
ALAN: Do you have girls behind her back?
DYSART: No.
ALAN: Then what? Do you fuck her?
DYSART: That's enough now.
He rises and moves away.
ALAN: Come on, tell me! Tell me, tell me!
DYSART: I said that's enough now.
Alan rises too and walks around him.
I bet you don't. I bet you never touch her. Come on, tell me. You've got no kids, have you? Is that because you don't fuck?
DYSART: [*sharp*] Go to your room. Go on: quick march.
Pause. Alan moves away from him, insolently takes up a packet of Dysart's cigarettes from the bench, and extracts one.

58

Give me those cigarettes.

The boy puts one in his mouth.

[*exploding*] Alan, *give them to me !*

Reluctantly Alan shoves the cigarette back in the packet, turns and hands it to him.

Now go !

Alan bolts out of the square, and back to his bed. Dysart, unnerved, addresses the audience.

Brilliant! Absolutely brilliant! The boy's on the run, so he gets defensive. What am *I*, then ? . . . Wicked little bastard – he knew exactly what questions to try. He'd actually marched himself round the hospital, making enquiries about my wife. Wicked and – of course, perceptive. Ever since I made that crack about carving up children, he's been aware of me in an absolutely specific way. Of course, there's nothing novel in that. Advanced neurotics can be dazzling at that game. They aim unswervingly at your area of maximum vulnerability . . . Which I suppose is as good a way as any of describing Margaret.

He sits. Hesther enters the square.

Light grows warmer.

18.

HESTHER: Now stop it.

DYSART. Do I embarrass you ?

HESTHER: I suspect you're about to.

Pause.

DYSART: My wife doesn't understand me, Your Honour.

HESTHER: Do you understand her ?

DYSART: No. Obviously I never did.

HESTHER: I'm sorry. I've never liked to ask but I've always imagined you weren't exactly compatible.

She moves to sit opposite.

DYSART: We were. It actually worked for a bit. I mean for both of us. We worked for each other. She actually for me through a kind of briskness. A clear, red-headed, inaccessible briskness which kept me keyed up for months. Mind you, if you're kinky for Northern Hygenic, as I am, you can't find anything much more compelling than a Scottish Lady Dentist.

HESTHER: It's *you* who are wicked, you know!

DYSART: Not at all: She got exactly the same from me. Antiseptic proficiency. I was like that in those days. We suited each other admirably. I see us in our wedding photo: Doctor and Doctor Mac Brisk. We were brisk in our wooing, brisk in our wedding, brisk in our disappointment. We turned from each other briskly into our separate surgeries: and now there's damn all.

HESTHER: You have no children, have you?

DYSART: No, we didn't go in for them. Instead, she sits beside our salmon-pink, glazed brick fireplace, and knits things for orphans in a home she helps with. And I sit opposite, turning the pages of art books on Ancient Greece. Occasionally, I still trail a faint scent of my enthusiasm across her path. I pass her a picture of the sacred acrobats of Crete leaping through the horns of running bulls – and she'll say: 'Och, Martin, what an *absurred* thing to be doing! The Highland Games, now there's *norrmal* sport!' Or she'll observe, just after I've told her a story from the Iliad: 'You know, when you come to think of it, Agamemnon and that lot were nothing but a bunch of ruffians from the Gorbals, only with fancy names!' [*He rises*] You get the picture. She's turned into a Shrink. The familiar domestic monster. Margaret Dysart: the Shrink's Shrink.

HESTHER: That's cruel, Martin.

DYSART: Yes. Do you know what it's like for two people to live in the same house as if they were in different parts of the world? Mentally, she's always in some drizzly kirk of her own inheriting: and I'm in some Doric temple – clouds tearing through pillars – eagles bearing prophecies out of the sky. She finds all that repulsive. All my wife has ever taken from the Mediterranean – from that whole vast intuitive culture – are four bottles of Chianti to make into lamps, and two china condiment donkeys labelled Sally and Peppy.

60

Pause.

[*more intimately*] I wish there was one person in my life I could show. One instinctive, absolutely unbrisk person I could take to Greece, and stand in front of certain shrines and sacred streams and say 'Look! Life is only comprehensible through a thousand local Gods. And not just the old dead ones with names like Zeus – no, but living Geniuses of Place and Person! And not just Greece but modern England! Spirits of certain trees, certain curves of brick wall, certain chip shops, if you like, and slate roofs – just as of certain frowns in people and slouches . . . I'd say to them – 'Worship as many as you can see – and more will appear!' . . . If I had a son, I bet you he'd come out exactly like his mother. Utterly worshipless. Would you like a drink?

HESTHER: No, thanks. Actually, I've got to be going. As usual . . .

DYSART: Really?

HESTHER: Really. I've got an Everest of papers to get through before bed.

DYSART: You never stop, do you?

HESTHER: Do you?

DYSART: This boy, with his stare. He's trying to save himself through me.

HESTHER: I'd say so.

DYSART: What am I trying to do to him?

HESTHER: Restore him, surely?

DYSART: To what?

HESTHER: A normal life.

DYSART: Normal?

HESTHER: It still means something.

DYSART: Does it?

HESTHER: Of course.

DYSART: You mean a normal boy has one head: a normal head has two ears?

HESTHER: You know I don't.

DYSART: Then what else?

HESTHER: [*lightly*] Oh, stop it.

DYSART: No, what? You tell me.

61

HESTHER: [*rising: smiling*] I won't be put on the stand like this, Martin. You're really disgraceful! . . . [*Pause*] You know what I mean by a normal smile in a child's eyes, and one that isn't – even if I can't exactly define it. Don't you?

DYSART: Yes.

HESTHER: Then we have a duty to that, surely? Both of us.

DYSART: Touché. . . . I'll talk to you.

HESTHER: Dismissed?

DYSART: You said you had to go.

HESTHER: I do . . . [*she kisses his cheek*]. Thank you for what you're doing. . . . You're going through a rotten patch at the moment. I'm sorry . . . I suppose one of the few things one can do is simply hold on to priorities.

DYSART: Like what?

HESTHER: Oh – children before grown-ups. Things like that.

He contemplates her.

DYSART: You're really quite splendid.

HESTHER: Famous for it. Goodnight.

She leaves him.

DYSART: [*to himself – or to the audience*] Normal! . . . Normal!

19.

Alan rises and enters the square. He is subdued.

DYSART: Good afternoon.

ALAN: Afternoon.

DYSART: I'm sorry about our row yesterday.

ALAN: It was stupid.

DYSART: It was.

ALAN: What I said, I mean.

DYSART: How are you sleeping?

Alan shrugs.

You're not feeling well, are you?

ALAN: All right.

DYSART: Would you like to play a game? It could make you feel better.

ALAN: What kind?

DYSART: It's called *Blink*. You have to fix your eyes on something: say, that little stain over there on the wall – and I tap this pen on the desk. The first time I tap it, you close your eyes. The next time you open them. And so on. Close, open, close, open, till I say Stop.

ALAN: How can that make you feel better?

DYSART: It relaxes you. You'll feel as though you're talking to me in your sleep.

ALAN: It's stupid.

DYSART: You don't have to do it, if you don't want to.

ALAN: I didn't say I didn't want to.

DYSART: Well?

ALAN: I don't mind.

DYSART: Good. Sit down and start watching that stain. Put your hands by your sides, and open the fingers wide.

He opens the left bench and Alan sits on the end of it.

The thing is to feel comfortable, and relax absolutely . . . Are you looking at the stain?

ALAN: Yes.

DYSART: Right. Now try and keep your mind as blank as possible.

ALAN: That's not difficult.

DYSART: Ssh. Stop talking . . . On the first tap, close. On the second, open. Are you ready?

Alan nods. Dysart taps his pen on the wooden rail. Alan shuts his eyes. Dysart taps again. Alan opens them. The taps are evenly spaced. After four of them the sound cuts out, and is replaced by a louder, metallic sound, on tape. Dysart talks through this, to the audience – the light changes to cold – while the boy sits in front of him, staring at the wall, opening and shutting his eyes.

The Normal is the good smile in a child's eyes – all right. It is also the dead stare in a million adults. It both sustains and kills – like a God. It is the Ordinary made beautiful: it is also the Average made lethal. The Normal is the indispensable, murderous God of Health, and I am his Priest. My tools are very delicate. My compassion is honest. I have honestly assisted children in this room. I have talked away terrors and

63

relieved many agonies. But also – beyond question – I have cut from them parts of individuality repugnant to this God, in both his aspects. Parts sacred to rarer and more wonderful Gods. And at what length . . . Sacrifices to Zeus took at the most, surely, sixty seconds each. Sacrifices to the Normal can take as long as sixty months.

The natural sound of the pencil resumes.
Light changes back.

[*to Alan*] Now your eyes are feeling heavy. You want to sleep, don't you? You want a long, deep sleep. Have it. Your head is heavy. Very heavy. Your shoulders are heavy. Sleep.

The pencil stops. Alan's eyes remain shut and his head has sunk on his chest.

Can you hear me?
ALAN: Mmm.
DYSART: You can speak normally. Say Yes, if you can.
ALAN: Yes.
DYSART: Good boy. Now raise your head, and open your eyes.
He does so.
Now, Alan, you're going to answer questions I'm going to ask you. Do you understand?
ALAN: Yes.
DYSART: And when you wake up, you are going to remember everything you tell me. All right?
ALAN: Yes.
DYSART: Good. Now I want you to think back in time. You are on that beach you told me about. The tide has gone out, and you're making sandcastles. Above you, staring down at you, is that great horse's head, and the cream dropping from it. Can you see that?
ALAN: Yes.
DYSART: You ask him a question. 'Does the chain hurt?'
ALAN: Yes.
DYSART: Do you ask him aloud?
ALAN: No.
DYSART: And what does the horse say back?
ALAN: 'Yes.'

DYSART: Then what do you say?
ALAN: 'I'll take it out for you.'
DYSART: And he says?
ALAN: 'It never comes out. They have me in chains.'
DYSART: Like Jesus?
ALAN: Yes!
DYSART: Only his name isn't Jesus, is it?
ALAN: No.
DYSART: What is it?
ALAN: No one knows but him and me.
DYSART: You can tell me, Alan. Name him.
ALAN: Equus.
DYSART: Thank you. Does he live in all horses or just some?
ALAN: All.
DYSART: Good boy. Now: you leave the beach. You're in your bedroom at home. You're twelve years old. You're in front of the picture. You're looking at Equus from the foot of your bed. Would you like to kneel down?
ALAN: Yes.
DYSART: [*encouragingly*] Go on, then.
    Alan kneels.
Now tell me. Why is Equus in chains?
ALAN: For the sins of the world.
DYSART: What does he say to you?
ALAN: 'I see you.' 'I will save you.'
DYSART: How?
ALAN: 'Bear you away. Two shall be one.'
DYSART: Horse and rider shall be one beast?
ALAN: One person!
DYSART: Go on.
ALAN: 'And my chinkle-chankle shall be in thy hand.'
DYSART: Chinkle-chankle? That's his mouth chain?
ALAN: Yes.
DYSART: Good. You can get up . . . Come on.
    Alan rises.
Now: think of the stable. What is the stable? His Temple? His Holy of Holies?
ALAN: Yes.

65

DYSART: Where you wash him? Where you tend him, and brush him with many brushes?

ALAN: Yes.

DYSART: And there he spoke to you, didn't he? He looked at you with his gentle eyes, and spake unto you?

ALAN: Yes.

DYSART: What did he say? 'Ride me?' 'Mount me, and ride me forth at night'?

ALAN: Yes.

DYSART: And you obeyed?

ALAN: Yes.

DYSART: How did you learn? By watching others?

ALAN: Yes.

DYSART: It must have been difficult. You bounced about?

ALAN: Yes.

DYSART: But he showed you, didn't he? Equus showed you the way.

ALAN: No!

DYSART: He didn't?

ALAN: He showed me nothing! He's a mean bugger! Ride – or fall! That's Straw Law.

DYSART: Straw Law?

ALAN: He was born in the straw, and this is his law.

DYSART: But you managed? You mastered him?

ALAN: Had to!

DYSART: And then you rode in secret?

ALAN: Yes.

DYSART: How often?

ALAN: Every three weeks. More, people would notice.

DYSART: On a particular horse?

ALAN: No.

DYSART: How did you get into the stable?

ALAN: Stole a key. Had it copied at Bryson's.

DYSART: Clever boy.

Alan smiles.

Then you'd slip out of the house?

ALAN: Midnight! On the stroke!

DYSART: How far's the stable?

ALAN: Two miles.
Pause.
DYSART: Let's do it! Let's go riding! ... Now!
He stands up, and pushes in his bench.
You are there now, in front of the stable door.
Alan turns upstage.
That key's in your hand. Go and open it.

20.

Alan moves upstage, and mimes opening the door.
Soft light on the circle.
Humming from the Chorus: the Equus noise.
The horse actors enter, raise high their masks, and put them on all together. They stand around the circle – Nugget in the mouth of the tunnel.
DYSART: Quietly as possible. Dalton may still be awake. Sssh ... Quietly ... Good. Now go in.
Alan steps secretly out of the square through the central opening on to the circle, now glowing with a warm light. He looks about him. The horses stamp uneasily: their masks turn towards him.
You are on the inside now. All the horses are staring at you. Can you see them?
ALAN: [*excited*] Yes!
DYSART: Which one are you going to take?
ALAN: Nugget.
Alan reaches up and mimes leading Nugget carefully round the circle downstage with a rope, past all the horses on the right.
DYSART: What colour is Nugget?
ALAN: Chestnut.
The horse picks his way with care. Alan halts him at the corner of the square.
DYSART: What do you do, first thing?
ALAN: Put on his sandals.
DYSART: Sandals?

He kneels, downstage centre.

ALAN: Sandals of majesty! . . . Made of sack.

He picks up the invisible sandals, and kisses them devoutly.

Tie them round his hooves.

He taps Nugget's right leg: the horse raises it and the boy mimes tying the sack round it.

DYSART: All four hooves?

ALAN: Yes.

DYSART: Then?

ALAN: Chinkle-chankle.

He mimes picking up the bridle and bit.

He doesn't like it so late, but he takes it for my sake. He bends for me. He stretches forth his neck to it.

Nugget bends his head down. Alan first ritually puts the bit into his own mouth, then crosses, and transfers it into Nugget's. He reaches up and buckles on the bridle. Then he leads him by the invisible reins, across the front of the stage and up round the left side of the circle. Nugget follows obediently.

ALAN: Buckle and lead out.

DYSART: No saddle?

ALAN: Never.

DYSART: Go on.

ALAN: Walk down the path behind. He's quiet. Always is, this bit. Meek and mild legs. At least till the field. Then there's trouble.

The horse jerks back. The mask tosses.

DYSART: What kind?

ALAN: Won't go in.

DYSART: Why not?

ALAN: It's his place of Ha Ha.

DYSART: What?

ALAN: Ha Ha.

DYSART: Make him go into it.

ALAN: [*whispering fiercely*] Come on! . . . Come on! . . .

He drags the horse into the square as Dysart steps out of it.

Nugget comes to a halt staring diagonally down what is now the field. The Equus noise dies away. The boy looks about him.

DYSART: [*from the circle*] Is it a big field?

ALAN: Huge!

DYSART: What's it like?

ALAN: Full of mist. Nettles on your feet.

He mimes taking off his shoes – and the sting.

Ah!

DYSART: [*going back to his bench*] You take your shoes off?

ALAN: Everything.

DYSART: All your clothes?

ALAN: Yes.

He mimes undressing completely in front of the horse. When he is finished, and obviously quite naked, he throws out his arms and shows himself fully to his God, bowing his head before Nugget.

DYSART: Where do you leave them?

ALAN: Tree hole near the gate. No one could find them.

He walks upstage and crouches by the bench, stuffing the invisible clothes beneath it. Dysart sits again on the left bench, downstage beyond the circle.

DYSART: How does it feel now?

ALAN: [*holds himself*] Burns.

DYSART: Burns?

ALAN: The mist!

DYSART: Go on. Now what?

ALAN: The Manbit.

He reaches again under the bench and draws out an invisible stick.

DYSART: Manbit?

ALAN: The stick for my mouth.

DYSART: Your mouth?

ALAN: To bite on.

DYSART: Why? What for?

ALAN: So's it won't happen too quick.

DYSART: Is it always the same stick?

ALAN: Course. Sacred stick. Keep it in the hole. The Ark of the Manbit.

DYSART: And now what?... What do you do now?

Pause. He rises and approaches Nugget.

ALAN: Touch him!

DYSART: Where?

ALAN: [*in wonder*] All over. Everywhere. Belly. Ribs. His ribs are of ivory. Of great value!... His flank is cool. His nostrils open for me. His eyes shine. They can see in the dark... *Eyes!*—

Suddenly he dashes in distress to the farthest corner of the square.

DYSART: *Go on!...* Then?

Pause.

ALAN: Give sugar.

DYSART: A lump of sugar?

Alan returns to Nugget.

ALAN: His Last Supper.

DYSART: Last before what?

ALAN: Ha Ha.

He kneels before the horse, palms upward and joined together.

DYSART: Do you say anything when you give it to him?

ALAN: [*offering it*] Take my sins. Eat them for my sake... He always does.

Nugget bows the mask into Alan's palm, then takes a step back to eat.

And then he's ready?

DYSART: You can get up on him now?

ALAN: Yes!

DYSART: Do it, then. Mount him.

Alan, lying before Nugget, stretches out on the square. He grasps the top of the thin metal pole embedded in the wood. He whispers his God's name ceremonially.

ALAN: Equus!... Equus!... Equus!

He pulls the pole upright. The actor playing Nugget leans

forward and grabs it. At the same instant all the other horses lean forward around the circle, each placing a gloved hand on the rail. Alan rises and walks right back to the upstage corner, left.

Take me !

He runs and jumps high on to Nugget's back.

[*crying out*] Ah !

DYSART: What is it ?

ALAN: Hurts!

DYSART: Hurts ?

ALAN: Knives in his skin! Little knives – all inside my legs.

Nugget mimes restiveness.

ALAN: Stay, Equus. No one said Go! . . . That's it. He's good. Equus the Godslave, Faithful and True. Into my hands he commends himself – naked in his chinkle-chankle. [*he punches* Stop it! . . . He wants to go so badly.

DYSART: Go, then. Leave me behind. Ride away now, Alan. Now! . . . Now you are alone with Equus.

Alan stiffens his body.

ALAN: [*ritually*] Equus – son of Fleckwus – son of Neckwus – Walk.

A hum from the Chorus.

Very slowly the horses standing on the circle begin to turn the square by gently pushing the wooden rail. Alan and his mount start to revolve. The effect, immediately, is of a statue being slowly turned round on a plinth. During the ride however the speed increases, and the light decreases until it is only a fierce spotlight on horse and rider, with the overspill glinting on the other masks leaning in towards them.

Here we go. The King rides out on Equus, mightiest of horses. Only I can ride him. He lets me turn him this way and that. His neck comes out of my body. It lifts in the dark. Equus, my Godslave! . . . Now the King commands you. Tonight, we ride against them all.

DYSART: Who's all ?

ALAN: My foes and His.

DYSART: Who are your foes ?

71

ALAN: The Hosts of Hoover. The Hosts of Philco. The Hosts of Pifco. The House of Remington and all its tribe!

DYSART: Who are His foes?

ALAN: The Hosts of Jodhpur. The Hosts of Bowler and Gymkhana. All those who show him off for their vanity. Tie rosettes on his head for their vanity! Come on, Equus. Let's get them!... *Trot!*

The speed of the turning square increases.

Stead-y! Stead-y! Stead-y! Stead-y! Cowboys are watching! Take off their stetsons. They know who we are. They're admiring us! Bowing low unto us! Come on now – show them! *Canter!* ... CANTER!

He whips Nugget.

And Equus the Mighty rose against All!

His enemies scatter, his enemies fall!

TURN!

Trample them, trample them,

Trample them, trample them,

TURN!

TURN!!

TURN!!!

The Equus noise increases in volume.

[*shouting*] WEE!... WAA!... WONDERFUL!...

I'm stiff! Stiff in the wind!

My mane, stiff in the wind!

My flanks! *My* hooves!

Mane on my legs, on my flanks, like whips!

Raw!

Raw!

I'm raw! Raw!

Feel me on you! *On* you! *On* you! *On* you!

I want to be *in* you!

I want to BE you forever and ever! –

Equus, I love you!

Now! –

Bear me away!

Make us One Person!

He rides Equus frantically.

72

One Person! One Person! One Person! One Person!
He rises up on the horse's back, and calls like a trumpet.
Ha-HA!...Ha-HA!...Ha-HA!
The trumpet turns to great cries.
HA-HA! HA-HA! HA-HA! HA-HA! HA!... HA!...
HAAAAA!
He twists like a flame.
Silence.
The turning square comes to a stop in the same position it occupied at the opening of the Act.
Slowly the boy drops off the horse's back on to the ground.
He lowers his head and kisses Nugget's hoof.
Finally he flings back his head and cries up to him:
AMEN!
Nugget snorts, once.

BLACKOUT

ACT TWO

22.

Darkness.

Lights come slowly up on Alan kneeling in the night at the hooves of Nugget. Slowly he gets up, climbing lovingly up the body of the horse until he can stand and kiss it.

Dysart sits on the downstage bench where he began Act One.

DYSART: With one particular horse, called Nugget, he embraces. He showed me how he stands with it afterwards in the night, one hand on its chest, one on its neck, like a frozen tango dancer, inhaling its cold sweet breath. 'Have you noticed,' he said, 'about horses: how they'll stand one hoof on its end, like those girls in the ballet?'

Alan leads Nugget out of the square. Dysart rises. The horse walks away up the tunnel and disappears. The boy comes downstage and sits on the bench Dysart has vacated. Dysart crosses downstage and moves slowly up round the circle, until he reaches the central entrance to the square.

Now he's gone off to rest, leaving me alone with Equus. I can hear the creature's voice. It's calling me out of the black cave of the Psyche. I shove in my dim little torch, and there he stands – waiting for me. He raises his matted head. He opens his great square teeth, and says – [*mocking*] '*Why?* . . . Why Me? . . . Why – ultimately – Me? . . . Do you really imagine you can account for Me? Totally, infallibly, inevitably account for Me? . . . Poor Doctor Dysart!'

He enters the square.

Of course I've stared at such images before. Or been stared at by them, whichever way you look at it. And weirdly often now with me the feeling is that *they* are staring at *us* – that in some quite palpable way they precede us. Meaningless, but unsettling . . . In either case, this one is the most alarming

74

yet. It asks questions I've avoided all my professional life. [*Pause*] A child is born into a world of phenomena all equal in their power to enslave. It sniffs – it sucks – it strokes it eyes over the whole uncomfortable range. Suddenly one strikes. Why? Moments snap together like magnets, forging a chain of shackles. Why? I can trace them. I can even, with time, pull them apart again. But why at the start they were ever magnetized at all – just those particular moments of experience and no others – I don't know. *And nor does anyone else.* Yet *if* I don't know – if I can never know that – then what am I doing here? I don't mean clinically doing or socially doing – I mean *fundamentally!* These questions, these Whys, are fundamental – yet they have no place in a consulting room. So then, do I? . . . This is the feeling more and more with me – No Place. Displacement. . . . 'Account for me,' says staring Equus. 'First account for Me! . . .' I fancy this is more than menopause.

Nurse rushes in.

NURSE: Doctor! . . . Doctor! There's a terrible scene with the Strang boy. His mother came to visit him, and I gave her the tray to take in. He threw it at her. She's saying the most dreadful things.

Alan springs up, down left. Dora springs up, down right. They face each other across the bottom end of the stage. It is observable that at the start of this Act Frank is not sitting beside his wife on their bench. It is hopefully not observable that he is placed among the audience upstage, in the gloom, by the central tunnel.

DORA: Don't you dare! *Don't you dare!*

DYSART: Is she still there?

NURSE: Yes!

He quickly leaves the square, followed by the Nurse. Dora moves towards her son.

DORA: Don't you look at me like that! I'm not a doctor, you know, who'll take anything. Don't you dare give me that stare, young man!

She slaps his face. Dysart joins them.

DYSART: Mrs Strang!

75

DORA: I know your stares. They don't work on me!
DYSART: [*to her*] Leave this room.
DORA: What did you say?
DYSART: I tell you to leave here at once.
  Dora hesitates. Then:
DORA: Goodbye, Alan.
  She walks past her son, and round into the square. Dysart
  follows her. Both are very upset. Alan returns to his
  bench and Nurse to her place.

23.

Lights up on the square.
DYSART: I must ask you never to come here again.
DORA: Do you think I want to? Do you think I want to?
DYSART: Mrs Strang, what on earth has got into you? Can't
  you see the boy is highly distressed?
DORA: [*ironic*] Really?
DYSART: Of course! He's at a most delicate stage of treatment.
  He's totally exposed. Ashamed. Everything you can imagine!
DORA: [*exploding*] *And me? What about me?* . . . *What do you*
  think I am? . . . I'm a parent, of course – so it doesn't count.
  That's a dirty word in here, isn't it, 'parent'?
DYSART: You know that's not true.
DORA: Oh, I know. I know, all right! I've heard it all my life.
  It's *our* fault. Whatever happens, *we* did it. Alan's just a
  little victim. He's really done nothing at all! [*savagely*] What
  do you have to do in this world to get any sympathy – blind
  animals?
DYSART: Sit down, Mrs Strang.
DORA: [*ignoring him: more and more urgently*] Look, Doctor:
  you don't have to live with this. Alan is one patient to you:
  one out of many. He's my son. I lie awake every night thinking about it. Frank lies there beside me. I can hear him.
  Neither of us sleeps all night. You come to us and say Who
  forbids television? who does what behind whose back? – as

if we're criminals. Let me tell you something. We're not criminals. We've done nothing wrong. We loved Alan. We gave him the best love we could. All right, we quarrel sometimes – all parents quarrel – we always make it up. My husband is a good man. He's an upright man, religion or no religion. He cares for his home, for the world, and for his boy. Alan had love and care and treats, and as much fun as any boy in the world. I know about loveless homes: I was a teacher. Our home wasn't loveless. I know about privacy too – not invading a child's privacy. All right, Frank may be at fault there – he digs into him too much – but nothing in excess. He's not a bully . . . [*gravely*] No, doctor. Whatever's happened has happened *because of Alan*. Alan is himself. Every soul is itself. If you added up everything we ever did to him, from his first day on earth to this, you wouldn't find why he did this terrible thing – because that's *him*: not just all of our things added up. Do you understand what I'm saying? I want you to understand, because I lie awake and awake thinking it out, and I want you to know that I deny it absolutely what he's doing now, staring at me, attacking me for what *he's* done, for what *he* is! [*pause: calmer*] You've got your words, and I've got mine. You call it a complex, I suppose. But if you knew God, Doctor, you would know about the Devil. You'd know the Devil isn't made by what mummy says and daddy says. The Devil's *there*. It's an old-fashioned word, but a true thing . . . I'll go. What I did in there was inexcusable. I only know he was my little Alan, and then the Devil came.

She leaves the square, and resumes her place. Dysart watches her go, then leaves himself by the opposite entrance, and approaches Alan.

24.

Seated on his bench, the boy glares at him.
DYSART: I thought you liked your mother.
Silence.

77

She doesn't know anything, you know. I haven't told her what you told me. You do know that, don't you?

ALAN: It was lies anyway.

DYSART: What?

ALAN: You and your pencil. Just a con trick, that's all.

DYSART: What do you mean?

ALAN: Made me say a lot of lies.

DYSART: Did it?... Like what?

ALAN: All of it. Everything I said. Lot of lies.

Pause.

DYSART: I see.

ALAN: You ought to be locked up. Your bloody tricks.

DYSART: I thought you liked tricks.

ALAN: It'll be the drug next. I know.

Dysart turns, sharply.

DYSART: What drug?

ALAN: I've heard. I'm not ignorant. I know what you get up to in here. Shove needles in people, pump them full of truth drug, so they can't help saying things. That's next, isn't it?

Pause.

DYSART: Alan, do you know why you're here?

ALAN: So you can give me truth drugs.

He glares at him.

Dysart leaves abruptly, and returns to the square.

25.

Hesther comes in simultaneously from the other side.

DYSART: [*agitated*] He actually thinks they exist! And of course he wants one.

HESTHER: It doesn't sound like that to me.

DYSART: Of course he does. Why mention them otherwise? He wants a way to speak. To finally tell me what happened in that stable. Tape's too isolated, and hypnosis is a trick. At least that's the pretence.

HESTHER: Does he still say that today?

DYSART: I haven't seen him. I cancelled his appointment this

78

morning, and let him stew in his own anxiety. Now I am almost tempted to play a real trick on him.

HESTHER: [*sitting*] Like what?

DYSART: The old placebo.

HESTHER: You mean a harmless pill?

DYSART: Full of *alleged* Truth Drug. Probably an aspirin.

HESTHER: But he'd deny it afterwards. Same thing all over.

DYSART: No. Because he's ready to abreact.

HESTHER: Abreact?

DYSART: Live it all again. He won't be able to deny it after that, because he'll have shown me. Not just told me – but acted it out in front of me.

HESTHER: Can you get him to do that?

DYSART: I think so. He's nearly done it already. Under all that glowering, he trusts me. Do you realise that?

HESTHER: [*warmly*] I'm sure he does.

DYSART: Poor bloody fool.

HESTHER: Don't start that again.

Pause.

DYSART: [*quietly*] Can you think of anything worse one can do to anybody than take away their worship?

HESTHER: Worship?

DYSART: Yes, that word again!

HESTHER: Aren't you being a little extreme?

DYSART: Extremity's the point.

HESTHER: Worship isn't destructive, Martin. I know that.

DYSART: I don't. I only know it's the core of his life. What else has he got? Think about him. He can hardly read. He knows no physics or engineering to make the world real for him. No paintings to show him how others have enjoyed it. No music except television jingles. No history except tales from a desperate mother. No friends. Not one kid to give him a joke, or make him know himself more moderately. He's a modern citizen for whom society doesn't exist. He lives *one hour* every three weeks – howling in a mist. And after the service kneels to a slave who stands over him obviously and unthrowably his master. With my body I thee worship! . . . Many men have less vital with their wives.

79

Pause.

HESTHER: All the same, they don't usually blind their wives, do they?

DYSART: Oh, come on!

HESTHER: Well, do they?

DYSART: [*sarcastically*] You mean he's dangerous? A violent, dangerous madman who's going to run round the country doing it again and again?

HESTHER: I mean he's in pain, Martin. He's been in pain for most of his life. That much, at least, you *know*.

DYSART: Possibly.

HESTHER: *Possibly?!* . . . That cut-off little figure you just described must have been in pain for years.

DYSART: [*doggedly*] Possibly.

HESTHER: And you can take it away.

DYSART: Still – possibly.

HESTHER: Then that's enough. That simply has to be enough for you, surely?

DYSART: No!

HESTHER: Why not?

DYSART: Because it's his.

HESTHER: I don't understand.

DYSART: His pain. His own. He made it.

Pause.

[*earnestly*] Look . . . to go through life and call it yours – *your life* – you first have to get your own pain. Pain that's unique to you. You can't just dip into the common bin and say 'That's enough!' . . . He's done that. All right, he's sick. He's full of misery and fear. He was dangerous, and could be again, though I doubt it. But that boy has known a passion more ferocious than I have felt in any second of my life. And let me tell you something: I envy it.

HESTHER: You can't.

DYSART: [*vehemently*] Don't you see? That's the Accusation! That's what his stare has been saying to me all this time. '*At least I galloped! When did you?*' . . . [*simply*] I'm jealous, Hesther. Jealous of Alan Strang.

HESTHER: That's absurd.

80

DYSART: Is it? . . . I go on about my wife. That smug woman by the fire. Have you thought of the fellow on the other side of it? The finicky, critical husband looking through his art books on mythical Greece. What worship has *he* ever known? Real worship! Without worship you shrink, it's as brutal as that . . . I shrank my *own* life. No one can do it for you. I settled for being pallid and provincial, out of my own eternal timidity. The old story of bluster, and do bugger-all . . . I imply that we can't have children: but actually, it's only me. I had myself tested behind her back. The lowest sperm count you could find. And I never told her. That's all I need – her sympathy mixed with resentment . . . I tell everyone Margaret's the puritan, I'm the pagan. Some pagan! Such wild returns I make to the womb of civilization. Three weeks a year in the Peleponnese, every bed booked in advance, every meal paid for by vouchers, cautious jaunts in hired Fiats, suitcase crammed with Kao-Pectate! Such a fantastic surrender to the primitive. And I use that word endlessly: 'primitive'. 'Oh, the primitive world,' I say. 'What instinctual truths were lost with it!' And while I sit there, baiting a poor unimaginative woman with the word, that freaky boy tries to conjure the reality! I sit looking at pages of centaurs trampling the soil of Argos—and outside my window he is trying to *become one*, in a Hampshire field! . . . I watch that woman knitting, night after night – a woman I haven't *kissed* in six years – and he stands in the dark for an hour, sucking the sweat off his God's hairy cheek! [*pause*] Then in the morning, I put away my books on the cultural shelf, close up the kodachrome snaps of Mount Olympus, touch my reproduction statue of Dionysus for luck – and go off to hospital to treat him for insanity. Do you see?

HESTHER: The boy's in pain, Martin. That's all I see. In the end . . . I'm sorry.

He looks at her. Alan gets up from his bench and stealthily places an envelope in the left-hand entrance of the square, then goes back and sits with his back to the audience, as if watching television.

Hesther rises.

HESTHER: That stare of his. Have you thought it might not be accusing you at all?
DYSART: What then?
HESTHER: Claiming you.
DYSART: For what?
HESTHER: [*mischievously*] A new God.
Pause.
DYSART: Too conventional, for him. Finding a religion in Psychiatry is really for very ordinary patients.
She laughs.
HESTHER: Maybe he just wants a new Dad. Or is that too conventional too? . . . Since you're questioning your profession anyway, perhaps you ought to try it and see.
DYSART: [*amused*] I'll talk to you.
HESTHER: Goodbye.
She smiles, and leaves him.

26.

Dysart becomes aware of the letter lying on the floor. He picks it up, opens and reads it.
ALAN: [*speaking stiffly, as Dysart reads*] 'It is all true, what I said after you tapped the pencil. I'm sorry if I said different. Post Scriptum: I know why I'm in here.'
Pause.
DYSART: [*calling, joyfully*] Nurse!
Nurse comes in.
NURSE: Yes, Doctor?
DYSART: [*trying to conceal his pleasure*] Good evening!
NURSE: You're in late tonight.
DYSART: Yes! . . . Tell me, is the Strang boy in bed yet?
NURSE: Oh, no, Doctor. He's bound to be upstairs looking at television. He always watches to the last possible moment. He doesn't like going to his room at all.
DYSART: You mean he's still having nightmares?
NURSE: He had a bad one last night.
DYSART: Would you ask him to come down here, please?

NURSE: [*faint surprise*] Now?

DYSART: I'd like a word with him.

NURSE: [*puzzled*] Very good, Doctor.

DYSART: If he's not back in his room by lights out, tell Night Nurse not to worry. I'll see he gets back to bed all right. And would you phone my home and tell my wife I may be in late?

NURSE: Yes, Doctor.

DYSART: Ask him to come straight away, please.

Nurse goes to the bench, taps Alan on the shoulder, whispers her message in his ear, and returns to her place. Alan stands up and pauses for a second – then steps into the square.

27.

He stands in the doorway, depressed.

DYSART: Hallo.

ALAN: Hallo.

DYSART: I got your letter. Thank you. [*pause*] Also the Post Scriptum.

ALAN: [*defensively*] That's the right word. My mum told me. It's Latin for 'After-writing'.

DYSART: How are you feeling?

ALAN: All right.

DYSART: I'm sorry I didn't see you today.

ALAN: You were fed up with me.

DYSART: Yes. [*pause*] Can I make it up to you now?

ALAN: What d'you mean?

DYSART: I thought we'd have a session.

ALAN: [*startled*] Now?

DYSART: Yes! At dead of night! . . . Better than going to sleep, isn't it?

The boy flinches.

Alan – look. Everything I say has a trick or a catch. Everything I do is a trick or a catch. That's all I know to do. But they work – and you know that. Trust me.

83

Pause.

ALAN: You got another trick, then?

DYSART: Yes.

ALAN: A truth drug?

DYSART: If you like.

ALAN: What's it do?

DYSART: Make it easier for you to talk.

ALAN: Like you can't help yourself?

DYSART: That's right. Like you have to speak the truth at all costs. And all of it.

Pause.

ALAN: [*slyly*] Comes in a needle, doesn't it?

DYSART: No.

ALAN: Where is it?

DYSART: [*indicating his pocket*] In here.

ALAN: Let's see.

Dysart solemnly takes a bottle of pills out of his pocket.

DYSART: There.

ALAN: [*suspicious*] That really it?

DYSART: It is ... Do you want to try it?

ALAN: No.

DYSART: I think you do.

ALAN: I don't. Not at all.

DYSART: Afterwards you'd sleep. You'd have no bad dreams all night. Probably many nights, from then on ...

Pause.

ALAN: How long's it take to work?

DYSART: It's instant. Like coffee.

ALAN: [*half believing*] It isn't!

DYSART: I promise you ... Well?

ALAN: Can I have a fag?

DYSART: Pill first. Do you want some water?

ALAN: No.

Dysart shakes one out on to his palm. Alan hesitates for a second – then takes it and swallows it.

DYSART: Then you can chase it down with this. Sit down.

He offers him a cigarette, and lights it for him.

ALAN: [*nervous*] What happens now?

84

DYSART: We wait for it to work.

ALAN: What'll I feel first?

DYSART: Nothing much. After a minute, about a hundred green snakes should come out of that cupboard singing the Hallelujah Chorus.

ALAN: [*annoyed*] *I'm serious!*

DYSART: [*earnestly*] You'll feel nothing. Nothing's going to happen now but what you want to happen. You're not going to say anything to me but what you want to say. Just relax. Lie back and finish your fag.

> *Alan stares at him. Then accepts the situation, and lies back.*

DYSART: Good boy.

ALAN: I bet this room's heard some funny things.

DYSART: It certainly has.

ALAN: I like it.

DYSART: This room?

ALAN: Don't you?

DYSART: Well, there's not much to like, is there?

ALAN: How long am I going to be in here?

DYSART: It's hard to say. I quite see you want to leave.

ALAN: No.

DYSART: You don't?

ALAN: Where would I go?

DYSART: Home. . . .

> *The boy looks at him. Dysart crosses and sits on the rail upstage, his feet on the bench. A pause.*

Actually, I'd like to leave this room and never see it again in my life.

ALAN: [*surprise*] Why?

DYSART: I've been in it too long.

ALAN: Where would you go?

DYSART: Somewhere.

ALAN: Secret?

DYSART: Yes. There's a sea – a great sea – I love . . . It's where the Gods used to go to bathe.

ALAN: What Gods?

DYSART: The old ones. Before they died.

85

ALAN: Gods don't die.
DYSART: Yes, they do.
> *Pause.*

There's a village I spent one night in, where I'd like to live.
It's all white.
ALAN: How would you Nosey Parker, though? You wouldn't
have a room for it any more.
DYSART: I wouldn't mind. I don't actually enjoy being a Nosey
Parker, you know.
ALAN: Then why do it?
DYSART: Because you're unhappy.
ALAN: So are you.
> *Dysart looks at him sharply. Alan sits up in alarm.*

Oooh, I didn't mean that!
DYSART: Didn't you?
ALAN: Here – is that how it works? Things just slip out, not
feeling anything?
DYSART: That's right.
ALAN: But it's so quick!
DYSART: I told you: it's instant.
ALAN: [*delighted*] It's wicked, isn't it? I mean, you can say
anything under it.
DYSART: Yes.
ALAN: Ask me a question.
DYSART: Tell me about Jill.
> *Pause. The boy turns away.*

ALAN: There's nothing to tell.
DYSART: Nothing?
ALAN: No.
DYSART: Well, for example – is she pretty? You've never
described her.
ALAN: She's all right.
DYSART: What colour hair?
ALAN: Dunno.
DYSART: Is it long or short?
ALAN: Dunno.
DYSART: [*lightly*] You must know that.
ALAN: I don't remember. *I don't!*

Dysart rises and comes down to him. He takes the cigarette out of his hand.
DYSART: [*firmly*] Lie back . . . Now listen. You have to do this. And now. You are going to tell me everything that happened with this girl. And not just *tell* me – *show* me. Act it out, if you like – even more than you did when I tapped the pencil. I want you to feel free to do absolutely anything in this room. The pill will help you. I will help you . . . Now, where does she live?
A long pause.
ALAN: [*tight*] Near the stables. About a mile.
Dysart steps down out of the square as Jill enters it. He sits again on the downstage bench.

28.

The light grows warmer.
JILL: It's called The China Pantry.
She comes down and sits casually on the rail. Her manner is open and lightly provocative. During these scenes Alan acts directly with her, and never looks over at Dysart when he replies to him.
When Daddy disappeared, she was left without a bean. She had to earn her own living. I must say she did jolly well, considering she was never trained in business.
DYSART: What do you mean, 'disappeared'?
ALAN: [*to Dysart*] He ran off. No one ever saw him again.
JILL: Just left a note on her dressing table saying 'Sorry. I've had it.' Just like that. She never got over it. It turned her right off men. All my dates have to be sort of secret. I mean, she knows about them, but I can't ever bring anyone back home. She's so rude to them.
ALAN: [*to Dysart*] She was always looking.
DYSART: At you?
ALAN: [*to Dysart*] Saying stupid things.
She jumps off the bench.
JILL: You've got super eyes.

87

ALAN: [*to Dysart*] Anyway, *she* was the one who had them.
She sits next to him. Embarassed, the boy tries to move away as far as he can.
JILL: There was an article in the paper last week saying what points about boys fascinate girls. They said Number One is bottoms. I think it's eyes every time ... They fascinate you too, don't they?
ALAN: Me?
JILL: [*sly*] Or is it only horse's eyes?
ALAN: [*startled*] What d'you mean?
JILL: I saw you staring into Nugget's eyes yesterday for ages. I spied on you through the door!
ALAN: [*hotly*] There must have been something in it!
JILL: You're a real Man of Mystery, aren't you?
ALAN: [*to Dysart*] Sometimes, it was like she knew.
DYSART: Did you ever hint?
ALAN: [*to Dysart*] Course not!
JILL: I love horses' eyes. The way you can see yourself in them. D'you find them sexy?
ALAN: [*outraged*] What?!
JILL: Horses.
ALAN: Don't be daft!
He springs up, and away from her.
JILL: Girls do. I mean, they go through a period when they pat them and kiss them a lot. I know *I* did. I suppose it's just a substitute, really.
ALAN: [*to Dysant*] That kind of thing, all the time. Until one night...
DYSART: Yes? What?
ALAN: [*to Dysart: defensively*] She did it! Not me. It was her idea, the whole thing!... She got me into it!
DYSART: What are you saying? 'One night': go on from there.
A pause.
ALAN: [*to Dysart*] Saturday night. We were just closing up.
JILL: How would you like to take me out?
ALAN: What?
JILL: [*coolly*] How would you like to take me out tonight?
ALAN: I've got to go home.

JILL: What for?
He tries to escape upstage.
ALAN: They expect me.
JILL: Ring up and say you're going out.
ALAN: I can't.
JILL: Why?
ALAN: They expect me.
JILL: Look. Either we go out together and have some fun, or
you go back to your boring home, *as usual*, and I go back to
mine. That's the situation, isn't it?
ALAN: Well... where would we go?
JILL: The pictures! There's a skinflick over in Winchester!
I've never seen one, have you?
ALAN: No.
JILL: Wouldn't you like to? *I* would. All those heavy Swedes,
panting at each other!... What d'you say?
ALAN: [*grinning*] Yeh!...
JILL: Good!...
He turns away.
DYSART: Go on, please.
He steps off the square.
ALAN: [*to Dysart*] I'm tired now!
DYSART: Come on now. You can't stop there.
*He storms round the circle to Dysart, and faces him
directly.*
ALAN: I'm *tired*! I want to go to bed!
DYSART: [*sharply*] Well, you can't. I want to hear about the
film.
ALAN: [*hostile*] Hear what?... *What?*... It was bloody
awful!
*The actors playing horses come swiftly on to the square,
dressed in sports coats or raincoats. They move the benches
to be parallel with the audience, and sit on them – staring
out front.*
DYSART: Why?
ALAN: Nosey Parker!
DYSART: *Why?*
ALAN: *Because!*.... Well – we went into the Cinema!

89

29

*A burst of Rock music, instantly fading down. Lights
darken.*

*Alan re-enters the square. Jill rises and together they grope
their way to the downstage bench, as if in a dark
auditorium.*

ALAN: [*To Dysart*] The whole place was full of men. Jill was
the only girl.

*They push by a patron seated at the end, and sit side by
side, staring up at the invisible screen, located above the
heads of the main audience. A spotlight hits the boy's face.*

We sat down and the film came on. It was daft. Nothing
happened for ages. There was this girl Brita, who was sixteen.
She went to stay in this house, where there was an older boy.
He kept giving her looks, but she ignored him completely. In
the end she took a shower. She went into the bathroom and
took off all her clothes. The lot. Very slowly. . . . What she
didn't know was the boy was looking through the door all the
time. . . . [*he starts to become excited*] It was fantastic! The
water fell on her breasts, bouncing down her. . . .

*Frank steps into the square furtively from the back, hat in
hand, and stands looking about for a place.*

DYSART: Was that the first time you'd seen a girl naked?

ALAN: [*to Dysart*] Yes! You couldn't see everything, though
. . . . [*looking about him*] All round me they were all looking.
All the men – staring up like they were in church. Like they
were a sort of congregation. And then – [*he sees his father*] *Ah!*

At the same instant Frank sees him.

FRANK: Alan!

ALAN: God!

JILL: What is it?

ALAN: *Dad!*

JILL: *Where?*

ALAN: At the back! *He saw me!*

JILL: You sure?

ALAN: Yes!

FRANK: [*calling*] Alan!

ALAN: Oh God!

> *He tries to hide his face in the girl's shoulder. His father comes down the aisle towards him.*

FRANK: Alan! You can hear me! Don't pretend!

PATRONS: *Sssh!*

FRANK: [*approaching the row of seats*] Do I have to come and fetch you out?...Do I?...

> *Cries of 'Sssh!' and 'Shut up!'*

Do I, Alan?

ALAN: [*through gritted teeth*] Oh fuck!

> *He gets up as the noise increases. Jill gets up too and follows him.*

DYSART: You went?

ALAN: [*to Dysart*] What else could I do? He kept shouting. Everyone was saying Shut up!

> *They go out, right, through the group of Patrons – who rise protesting as they pass, quickly replace the benches and leave the square.*
> *Dysart enters it.*

30.

> *Light brightens from the cinema, but remains cold: streets at night.*
> *The three walk round the circle downstage in a line: Frank leading, wearing his hat. He halts in the middle of the left rail, and stands staring straight ahead of him, rigid with embarassment.*
> *Alan is very agitated.*

ALAN: [*to Dysart*] We went into the street, all three of us. It was weird. We just stood there by the bus stop – like we were three people in a queue, and we didn't know each other. Dad was all white and sweaty. He didn't look at us at all. It must have gone on for about five minutes. I tried to speak. I said— [*to his father*] I – I – I've never been there before.

Honest . . . Never . . . [*to Dysart*] He didn't seem to hear. Jill tried.

JILL:It's true, Mr Strang. It wasn't Alan's idea to go there. It was mine.

ALAN: [*to Dysart*] He just went on staring, straight ahead. It was awful.

JILL: I'm not shocked by films like that. I think they're just silly.

ALAN: [*to Dysart*] The bus wouldn't come. We just stood and stood. . . . Then suddenly he spoke.

Frank takes off his hat.

FRANK: [*stiffly*] I'd like you to know something. Both of you. I came here tonight to see the Manager. He asked me to call on him for business purposes. I happen to be a printer, Miss. A picture house needs posters. That's entirely why I'm here. To discuss posters. While I was waiting I happened to glance in, that's all. I can only say I'm going to complain to the council. I had no idea they showed films like this. I'm certainly going to refuse my services.

JILL: [*kindly*] Yes, of course.

FRANK: So long as that's understood.

ALAN: [*to Dysart*] Then the bus came along.

FRANK: Come along, now Alan.

He moves away downstage.

ALAN: No.

FRANK: [*turning*] No fuss, please. Say Goodnight to the young lady.

ALAN: [*timid but firm*] No. I'm stopping here . . . I've got to see her home . . . It's proper.

Pause.

FRANK: [*as dignified as possible*] Very well. I'll see you when you choose to return. Very well then . . . Yes . . .

He walks back to his original seat, next to his wife. He stares across the square at his son – who stares back at him. Then, slowly, he sits.

ALAN: [*To Dysart*] And he got in, and we didn't. He sat down and looked at me through the glass. And I saw . . .

DYSART: [*soft*] What?

ALAN: [*to Dysart*] His face. It was scared.
DYSART: Of you?
ALAN: [*to Dysart*] It was terrible. We had to walk home. Four
miles. I got the shakes.
DYSART: You were scared too?
ALAN: [*to Dysart*] It was like a hole had been drilled in my
tummy. A hole – right here. And the air was getting in!
He starts to walk upstage, round the circle.

31.

The girl stays still.
JILL: [*aware of other people looking*] Alan . . .
ALAN: [*to Dysart*] People kept turning round in the street to
look.
JILL: Alan!
ALAN: [*to Dysart*] I kept seeing him, just as he drove off.
Scared of me. . . . And me scared of *him*. . . . I kept thinking
– all those airs he put on! . . . 'Receive my meaning. Improve
your mind!' . . . All those nights he said he'd be in late.
'Keep my supper hot, Dora!' 'Your poor father: he works so
hard!' . . . Bugger! Old bugger! . . . Filthy old bugger!
He stops, clenching his fists.
JILL: Hey! Wait for me!
She runs after him. He waits.
What are you thinking about?
ALAN: Nothing.
JILL: Mind my own beeswax?
She laughs.
ALAN: [*to Dysart*] And suddenly she began to laugh.
JILL: I'm sorry. But it's pretty funny, when you think of it.
ALAN: [*bewildered*] What?
JILL: Catching him like that! I mean, it's terrible – but it's very
funny.
ALAN: Yeh!
He turns from her.
JILL: No, wait! . . . I'm sorry. I know you're upset. But it's

93

not the end of the world, is it? I mean, what was he doing? Only what we were. Watching a silly film. It's a case of like father like son, I'd say! . . . I mean, when that girl was taking a shower, you were pretty interested, weren't you?

He turns round and looks at her.

We keep saying old people are square. Then when they suddenly aren't – we don't like it!

DYSART: What did you think about that?

ALAN: [*to Dysart*] I don't know. I kept looking at all the people in the street. They were mostly men coming out of pubs. I suddenly thought – *they all do it! All of them!* . . . They're not just Dads – they're people with pricks! . . . And Dad – he's just not Dad either. He's a man with a prick too. You know, I'd never thought about it.

Pause.

We went into the country.

He walks again. Jill follows. They turn the corner and come downstage, right.

We kept walking. I just thought about Dad, and how he was nothing special – just a poor old sod on his own.

He stops.

[*to Jill: realising it*] Poor old sod!

JILL: That's right!

ALAN: [*grappling with it*] I mean, what else has he got? . . . He's got mum, of course, but well – she – she—she——

JILL: She doesn't give him anything?

ALAN: That's right. I bet you . . . She doesn't give him anything. That's right . . . That's really right! . . . She likes Ladies and Gentlemen. Do you understand what I mean?

JILL: [*mischievously*] Ladies and gentlemen aren't naked?

ALAN: That's right! Never! . . . *Never!* That would be disgusting! She'd have to put bowler hats on them! . . . Jodhpurs!

She laughs.

DYSART: Was that the first time you ever thought anything like that about your mother? . . . I mean, that she was unfair to your dad?

ALAN: [*to Dysart*] Absolutely!

94

DYSART: How did you feel?

ALAN: [*to Dysart*] Sorry. I mean for him. Poor old sod, that's what I felt – he's just like me! He hates ladies and gents just like me! Posh things – and la-di-da. He goes off by himself at night, and does his own secret thing which no one'll know about, just like me! There's no difference – he's just the same as me – just the same!—

He stops in distress, then bolts back a little upstage.

Christ!

DYSART: [*sternly*] Go on.

ALAN: [*to Dysart*] I can't.

DYSART: Of course you can. You're doing wonderfully.

ALAN: [*to Dysart*] No, please. *Don't make me!*

DYSART: [*firm*] Don't think: just answer. You were happy at that second, weren't you? When you realised about your dad. How lots of people have secrets, not just you?

ALAN: [*to Dysart*] Yes.

DYSART: You felt sort of free, didn't you? I mean, free to do anything?

ALAN: [*to Dysart, looking at Jill*] Yes!

DYSART: What was she doing?

ALAN: [*to Dysart*] Holding my hand.

DYSART: And that was good?

ALAN: [*to Dysart*] Oh, yes!

DYSART: Remember what you thought. *As if it's happening to you now. This very moment* ... What's in your head?

ALAN: [*to Dysart*] Her eyes. *She's* the one with eyes! ... I keep looking at them, because I really want—

DYSART: To look at her breasts?

ALAN: [*to Dysart*] Yes.

DYSART: Like in the film.

ALAN: [*to Dysart*] Yes ... Then she starts to scratch my hand.

JILL: You're really very nice, you know that?

ALAN: [*to Dysart*] Moving her nails on the back. Her face so warm. Her eyes.

DYSART: You want her very much?

ALAN: [*to Dysart*] Yes ...

JILL: I love your eyes.

95

She kisses him.
[*whispering*] Let's go!
ALAN: Where?
JILL: I know a place. It's right near here.
ALAN: Where?
JILL: Surprise!... Come on!
    *She darts away round the circle, across the stage and up
    the left side.*
Come *on!*
ALAN: [*To Dysart*] She runs ahead. I follow. And then—and
then—!
    He halts.
DYSART: What?
ALAN: [*To Dysart*] I see what she means.
DYSART: What?... Where are you?... Where has she taken
you?
ALAN: [*to Jill*] The Stables?
JILL: Of course!

32.

Chorus makes a warning hum.
*The horses actors enter, and ceremonially put on their
masks – first raising them high above their heads. Nugget
stands in the central tunnel.*
ALAN: [*recoiling*] No!
JILL: Where else? They're perfect!
ALAN: No!
    He turns his head from her.
JILL: Or do you want to go home now and face your dad?
ALAN: No!
JILL: Then come on!
    *He edges nervously past the horse standing at the left, which
    turns its neck and even moves a challenging step after him.*
ALAN: Why not your place?
JILL: I can't. Mother doesn't like me bringing back boys. I
told you.... Anyway, the Barn's better.

96

ALAN: No!
JILL: All that straw. It's cosy.
ALAN: No.
JILL: *Why not?*
ALAN: Them!
JILL: Dalton will be in bed . . . What's the matter? . . . Don't you want to?
ALAN: [*aching to*] Yes!
JILL: So?
ALAN: [*desperate*] *Them! . . . Them! . . .*
JILL: *Who?*
ALAN: [*low*] Horses.
JILL: *Horses? . . .* You're really dotty, aren't you? . . . What do you mean?
He starts shaking.
Oh, you're freezing . . . Let's get under the straw. You'll be warm there.
ALAN: [*pulling away*] No!
JILL: What on earth's the matter with you? . . .
Silence. He won't look at her.
Look, if the sight of horses offends you, my lord, we can just shut the door. You won't have to see them. All right?
DYSART: What door is that? In the barn?
ALAN: [*to Dysart*] Yes.
DYSART: So what do you do? You go in?
ALAN: [*to Dysart*] Yes.

33.

A rich light falls.
Furtively Alan enters the square from the top end, and Jill follows. The horses on the circle retire out of sight on either side. Nugget retreats up the tunnel and stands where he can just be glimpsed in the dimness.
DYSART: Into the Temple? The Holy of Holies?
ALAN: [*to Dysart: desperate*] What else can I do? . . . I can't say! I can't tell her . . . [*to Jill*] Shut it tight.

97

JILL: All right . . . You're crazy!

ALAN: Lock it.

JILL: Lock?

ALAN: Yes.

JILL: It's just an old door. What's the matter with you? They're in their boxes. They can't get out . . . Are you all right?

ALAN: Why?

JILL: You look weird.

ALAN: *Lock it!*

JILL: Sssh! D'you want to wake up Dalton? . . . Stay there, idiot.

She mimes locking a heavy door, upstage.

DYSART: Describe the barn, please.

ALAN: [*walking round it: to Dysart*] Large room. Straw everywhere. Some tools . . . [*as if picking it up off the rail where he left it in Act One*] A hoof pick! . . .

He 'drops' it hastily, and dashes away from the spot.

DYSART: *Go on.*

ALAN: [*to Dysart*] At the end this big door. Behind it—

DYSART: Horses.

ALAN: [*to Dysart*] Yes.

DYSART: How many?

ALAN: [*to Dysart*] Six.

DYSART: Jill closes the door so you can't see them?

ALAN: [*to Dysart*] Yes.

DYSART: And then? . . . What happens now? . . . Come on, Alan. Show me.

JILL: See, it's all shut. There's just us . . . Let's sit down. Come on.

They sit together on the same bench, left.

Hallo.

ALAN: [*quickly*] Hallo.

She kisses him lightly. He responds. Suddenly a faint trampling of hooves, off-stage, makes him jump up.

JILL: What is it?

He turns his head upstage, listening.

Relax. There's no one there. Come here.

She touches his hand. He turns to her again.
You're very gentle. I love that ...
ALAN: So are you ... I mean ...
He kisses her spontaneously. The hooves trample again, harder. He breaks away from her abruptly towards the upstage corner.
JILL: [*rising*] What is it?
ALAN: Nothing!
She moves towards him. He turns and moves past her. He is clearly distressed. She contemplates him for a moment.
JILL: [*gently*] Take your sweater off.
ALAN: What?
JILL: I will, if you will.
He stares at her. A pause.
She lifts her sweater over head: he watches – then unzips his. They each remove their shoes, their socks, and their jeans. Then they look at each other diagonally across the square, in which the light is gently increasing.
ALAN: You're ... You're very ...
JILL: So are you. ... [*pause*] Come here.
He goes to her. She comes to him. They meet in the middle, and hold each other, and embrace.
ALAN: [*to Dysart*] She put her mouth in mine. It was lovely! *Oh, it was lovely!*
They burst into giggles. He lays her gently on the floor in the centre of the square, and bends over her eagerly.
Suddenly the noise of Equus fills the place. Hooves smash on wood. Alan straightens up, rigid. He stares straight ahead of him over the prone body of the girl.
DYSART: Yes, what happened then, Alan?
ALAN: [*to Dysart: brutally*] I put it in her!
DYSART: Yes?
ALAN: [*to Dysart*] I put it in her.
DYSART: You did?
ALAN: [*to Dysart*] Yes!
DYSART: Was it easy?
ALAN: [*to Dysart*] Yes.
DYSART: Describe it.

ALAN: [*to Dysart*] I told you.
DYSART: More exactly.
ALAN: [*to Dysart*] I put it in her!
DYSART: Did you?
ALAN: [*to Dysart*] All the way!
DYSART: Did you, Alan?
ALAN: [*to Dysart*] All the way. I shoved it. I put it in her all the way.
DYSART: Did you?
ALAN: [*to Dysart*] Yes!
DYSART: Did you?
ALAN: [*to Dysart*] Yes!... Yes!
DYSART: Give me the TRUTH!... Did you?... *Honestly?*
ALAN: [*to Dysart*] Fuck off!

He collapses, lying upstage on his face. Jill lies on her back motionless, her head downstage, her arms extended behind her. A pause.

DYSART: [*gently*] What was it? You couldn't? Though you wanted to very much?
ALAN: [*to Dysart*] I couldn't... see her.
DYSART: What do you mean?
ALAN: [*to Dysart*] Only Him. Every time I kissed her – *He* was in the way.
DYSART: Who?

Alan turns on his back.

ALAN: [*to Dysart*] You *know* who!... When I touched her, I felt *Him*. Under me... His side, waiting for my hand... His flanks... I refused him. I looked. I looked right at her... and I couldn't do it. When I shut my eyes, I saw Him at once. The streaks on his belly... [*with more desperation*] I couldn't feel *her* flesh at all! I wanted the foam off his neck. His sweaty hide. Not flesh. *Hide! Horse-hide!*... Then I couldn't even kiss her.

Jill sits up.

JILL: What is it?
ALAN: [*dodging her hand*] No!

He scrambles up and crouches in the corner against the rails, like a little beast in a cage.

JILL: Alan!
ALAN: Stop it!
Jill gets up.
JILL: It's all right . . . It's all right . . . Don't worry about it.
It often happens – honest. . . . There's nothing wrong. I
don't mind, you know . . . I don't at all.
He dashes past her downstage.
Alan, look at me . . . Alan ? . . . Alan!
He collapses again by the rail.
ALAN: Get out! . . .
JILL: What?
ALAN: [*soft*] Out!
JILL: There's nothing wrong: believe me! It's very common.
ALAN: *Get out!*
He snatches up the invisible pick.
GET OUT!
JILL: Put that down!
ALAN: Leave me alone!
JILL: Put that down, Alan. It's very dangerous. Go on, please –
drop it.
He 'drops' it, and turns from her.
ALAN: You ever tell anyone. Just you tell . . .
JILL: Who do you think I am ? . . . I'm your friend— Alan . . .
She goes towards him.
Listen: you don't have to do anything. Try to realize that.
Nothing at all. Why don't we just lie here together in the
straw. And talk.
ALAN: [*low*] Please . . .
JILL: Just talk.
ALAN: *Please!*
JILL: All right, I'm going . . . Let me put my clothes on first.
She dresses, hastily.
ALAN: You tell anyone! . . . Just tell and see. . . .
JILL: *Oh, stop it!* . . . I wish you could believe me. It's not in
the least important.
Pause.
Anyway, I won't say anything. You know that. You know I
won't. . . .

Pause. He stands with his back to her.
Goodnight, then, Alan. . . . I wish – I really wish—
He turns on her, hissing. His face is distorted – possessed.
In horrified alarm she turns – fumbles the door open –
leaves the barn – shuts the door hard behind her, and
dashes up the tunnel out of sight, past the barely visible
figure of Nugget.

34.

Alan stands alone, and naked.
A faint humming and drumming. The boy looks about him
in growing terror.
DYSART: What?
ALAN:[*to Dysart*] He was there. Through the door. The door
was shut, but he was there! . . . He'd seen everything. I could
hear him. He was laughing.
DYSART: Laughing?
ALAN: [*to Dysart*] Mocking! . . . *Mocking!* . . .
Standing downstage he stares up towards the tunnel. A
great silence weighs on the square.
[*To the silence: terrified*] Friend . . . Equus the Kind . . . The
Merciful! . . . *Forgive me!* . . .
Silence.
It wasn't me. Not really me. *Me!* . . . Forgive me! . . . Take
me back again! Please!... PLEASE!
He kneels on the downstage lip of the square, still facing
the door, huddling in fear.
I'll never do it again. I swear . . . I swear!...
Silence.
[*in a moan*] *Please ! ! !* . . .
DYSART: And He? What does He say?
ALAN: [*to Dysart: whispering*] 'Mine! . . . You're mine! . . . I
am yours and you are mine!' . . . Then I see his eyes. They
are rolling!
Nugget begins to advance slowly, with relentless hooves,
down the central tunnel.

'I see you. I see you. Always! Everywhere! Forever!'

DYSART: Kiss anyone and I will see?

ALAN: [to Dysart] Yes!

DYSART: Lie with anyone and I will see?

ALAN: [to Dysart] Yes!

DYSART: And you will fail! Forever and ever you will *fail!* You will see ME – and you will FAIL!

The boy turns round, hugging himself in pain. From the sides two more horses converge with Nugget on the rails. Their hooves stamp angrily. The Equus noise is heard more terribly.

The Lord thy God is a Jealous God. He sees you. He sees you forever and ever, Alan. He sees you! . . . *He sees you!*

ALAN: [in terror] Eyes! . . . White eyes – never closed! Eyes like flames – coming – coming! . . . God seest! God seest! . . . NO! . . .

Pause. He steadies himself. The stage begins to blacken.

[quieter] No more. No more, Equus.

He gets up. He goes to the bench. He takes up the invisible pick. He moves slowly upstage towards Nugget, concealing the weapon behind his naked back, in the growing darkness. He stretches out his hand and fondles Nugget's mask.

[gently] Equus . . . Noble Equus . . . Faithful and True . . . Godslave . . . Thou—God—Seest—NOTHING!

He stabs out Nugget's eyes. The horse stamps in agony. A great screaming begins to fill the theatre, growing ever louder. Alan dashes at the other two horses and blinds them too, stabbing over the rails. Their metal hooves join in the stamping.

Relentlessly, as this happens, three more horses appear in cones of light: not naturalistic animals like the first three, but dreadful creatures out of nightmare. Their eyes flare – their nostrils flare – their mouths flare. They are archetypal images – judging, punishing, pitiless. They do not halt at the rail, but invade the square. As they trample at him, the boy leaps desperately at them, jumping high and naked in the dark, slashing at their heads with arms upraised. The screams increase. The other horses follow into the square. The whole place is filled with cannoning, blinded horses – and the boy dodging among them, avoiding their slashing hooves as best he can. Finally they plunge off into darkness and away out of sight. The noise dies abruptly, and all we hear is Alan yelling in hysteria as he collapses on the ground – stabbing at his own eyes with the invisible pick.

ALAN: Find me! . . . Find me! . . . Find me! . . .
KILL ME! . . . KILL ME! . . .

35.

The light changes quickly back to brightness.
Dysart enters swiftly, hurls a blanket on the left bench, and rushes over to Alan. The boy is having convulsions on the floor. Dysart grabs his hands, forces them from his eyes, scoops him up in his arms and carries him over to the bench. Alan hurls his arms round Dysart and clings to him, gasping and kicking his legs in a dreadful frenzy.
Dysart lays him down and presses his head back on the bench. He keeps talking – urgently talking – soothing the agony as he can.

DYSART: Here . . . Here . . . Ssssh . . . Ssssh . . . Calm now . . . Lie back. *Just lie back!* Now breathe in deep. Very deep. In . . . Out . . . In . . . Out . . . That's it. . . . In. *Out . . . In . . . Out . . .*

The boy's breath is drawn into his body with a harsh rasping sound, which slowly grows less. Dysart puts the blanket over him.

Keep it going . . . That's a good boy . . . Very good boy . . . It's all over now, Alan. It's all over. He'll go away now. You'll never see him again, I promise. You'll have no more bad dreams. No more awful nights. Think of that! . . . You are going to be well. I'm going to make you well, I promise you. . . . You'll be here for a while, but I'll be here too, so it won't be so bad. Just trust me . . .

He stands upright. The boy lies still.

Sleep now. Have a good long sleep. You've earned it . . .

Sleep. Just sleep. . . . I'm going to make you well.
He steps backwards into the centre of the square. The light brightens some more.
A pause.
DYSART: I'm lying to you, Alan. He won't really go that easily. Just clop away from you like a nice old nag. Oh, no! When Equus leaves – if he leaves at all – it will be with your intestines in his teeth. And I don't stock replacements . . . If you knew anything, you'd get up this minute and run from me fast as you could.
Hesther speaks from her place.
HESTHER: The boy's in pain, Martin.
DYSART: Yes.
HESTHER: And you can take it away.
DYSART: Yes.
HESTHER: Then that has to be enough for you, surely? . . . In the end!
DYSART: [*crying out*] *All right! I'll take it away!* He'll be delivered from madness. *What then?* He'll feel himself acceptable! *What then?* Do you think feelings like his can be simply re-attached, like plasters? Stuck on to other objects we select? *Look at him!* . . . My desire might be to make this boy an ardent husband – a caring citizen – a worshipper of abstract and unifying God. My achievement, however, is more likely to make a ghost! . . . Let me tell you exactly what I'm going to do to him!
He steps out of the square and walks round the upstage end of it, storming at the audience.
I'll heal the rash on his body. I'll erase the welts cut into his mind by flying manes. When that's done, I'll set him on a nice mini-scooter and send him puttering off into the Normal world where animals are treated *properly*: made extinct, or put into servitude, or tethered all their lives in dim light, just to feed it! I'll give him the good Normal world where we're tethered beside them – blinking our nights away in a non-stop drench of cathode-ray over our shrivelling heads! I'll take away his Field of Ha Ha, and give him Normal places for his ecstasy – multi-lane highways driven through the guts

of cities, extinguishing Place altogether, *even the idea of Place!* He'll trot on his metal pony tamely through the concrete evening – and one thing I promise you: he will never touch hide again! With any luck his private parts will come to feel as plastic to him as the products of the factory to which he will almost certainly be sent. Who knows? He may even come to find sex funny. Smirky funny. Bit of grunt funny. Trampled and furtive and entirely in control. Hopefully, he'll feel nothing at his fork but Approved Flesh. *I doubt, however, with much passion!* . . . Passion, you see, can be destroyed by a doctor. It cannot be created.

He addresses Alan directly, in farewell.

You won't gallop any more, Alan. Horses will be quite safe. You'll save your pennies every week, till you can change that scooter in for a car, and put the odd fifty P on the gee-gees, quite forgetting that they were ever anything more to you than bearers of little profits and little losses. You will, however, be without pain. More or less completely without pain.

Pause.

He speaks directly to the theatre, standing by the motionless body of Alan Strang, under the blanket.

And now for me it never stops: that voice of Equus out of the cave – 'Why Me? . . . Why Me? . . . Account for Me!' . . . All right – I surrender! I say it! . . . In an ultimate sense I cannot know what I do in this place – yet I do ultimate things. Essentially I cannot know what I do – yet I do essential things. Irreversible, terminal things. I stand in the dark with a pick in my hand, striking at heads!

He moves away from Alan, back to the downstage bench, and finally sits.

I need – more desperately than my children need me – a way of seeing in the dark. What way is this? . . . *What dark is this?* . . . I cannot call it ordained of God: I can't get that far. I will however pay it so much homage. There is now, in my mouth, this sharp chain. And it never comes out.

A long pause.

Dysart sits staring.

BLACKOUT

106

SHRIVINGS

IN MEMORY
OF
JAMES MOSSMAN

A NOTE ON THE PLAY: 1974

As of now, this play has never been acted. It is a much re-written version of another play of mine called *The Battle of Shrivings*, which has never been printed. This first version was presented at the Lyric Theatre, London, in February 1970, by five fine actors: John Gielgud, Patrick Magee, Wendy Hiller, ebullient young Dorothy Lyman and compelling young Martin Shaw. It was directed with cool precision by Peter Hall, and placed by John Bury in a set so bone-white that a bowl of green apples placed suddenly on a table – 'the buttons of original sin' – rivetted every eye. The action of the play was lightly formalised throughout, so that it could make an austere gesture somewhat at variance with the aesthetic standards prevailing on Shaftesbury Avenue. I found this gesture beautiful, since my intention from the start had always been to stage a fairly abstract proceeding, and theatrically I am strongly drawn to the cold which burns. However, it is possible that the proceeding was not abstract enough, or not cold enough to burn effectively. At any rate the play fell somewhere between domesticity and grandeur – a bad kind of fall – and though some critics found it exciting, many more received it with an almost jubilant hostility.

For myself, the more I saw *The Battle of Shrivings* performed, the more I wanted to change it. I do not mean that I just wanted to make it work. 'Working', in the sense intended by many theatrical professionals, far too often simply means a certain effectiveness purchased at the price of any ambiguous insight, or of any qualifying perception not immediately accessible to a dozing audience sullenly suspicious of language. Other plays of mine had relied for their completion on elaborate stretches of physical action: in this one I wanted the electricity to be sparked almost exclusively from the spoken words – though of course there was a physical set-piece as well in the shape of the Apple Game. My dissatisfaction with the piece, therefore, had nothing to do with its rhetoric, which if anything

I wanted to intensify; nor with its verbal duelling, which if anything I wanted to extend. I desired only to make the play more purely *itself*.

Successful plays of large scope die for their authors with a pleasant expiration, wrapped in a sheet of public approval: unsuccessful ones are apt to be left naked to the sky – particularly plays of a turbulent nature – writhing under an obloquy which never quite covers them and so turns into oblivion. I remember how in the first hard weeks after its public maiming, I became obsessed with considering what further writing was needed to give the play its quietus in my mind. I had loved it a great deal, but had I allowed it to speak entirely in its own voice? I suspected that the intransigence of the argument had been blunted by an almost conventional turn it had taken, towards the end, into domestic bickering. Certain furious passages between the husband and the wife had been undeniably useful in humanising action otherwise largely concerned with debate, but I wondered whether fundamentally they had not constituted an easy way around the rigorous path which the piece should properly have followed. The first thing I did when I started to rewrite, was to remove altogether the character of Enid Petrie, the pacifist's unhappy wife, thereby changing a quintet into a quartet.

The creation of Lady Petrie in the first place had been largely due to some speculation I once entertained concerning the household of Mahatma Gandhi. I had read in a famous Life of the great man how at the age of forty he had summoned his wife and informed her of his irrevocable decision to give up all sexual activity, since he had come to recognize in it the source of aggression in himself. This startling act of renunciation certainly impressed me: but I could not stop wondering at the same time about the reaction to it of Mrs Gandhi. Her possible sufferings seemed so extremely relevant to my theme, and to the doings in the Petrie household. Indeed some years later I received a passionate letter from a woman psychiatrist, warmly congratulating me on perceiving how often idealism of the lofty Petrie kind is fed by the life-blood of humble domestic victims. However, despite my speculations about Gandhi's wife (and the encouraging letter from this doctor) I could not finally avoid the insistent conclusion that Enid Petrie was a dramatic cliché, and that the scene where she was finally struck by her husband was simply no fitting climax for the play. Obviously the horror of this story, in any version of it, has to be Gideon's lapse into violence after so many years of self-restraint. But with Enid removed, a more dramatically interesting target for the pacifist's blow instantly appeared: Lois, his idealistic and worshipping young secretary. An assault on a committed girl seemed to me in this situation even more appalling than one on an aggrieved wife. The fact that the girl was also an American clinched the matter for me.

Shrivings has always been an 'American' play. I associate it most strongly with sojourns in New York City in 1968 and 1969. The encounter between Mark and Gideon naturally sprang out of a division of feeling in myself, but it was charged with the violence of this angry city during one of her angriest times, when streets were choked with raging protesters against the Vietnam War, newspapers were filled with the killings at Kent State University, and there drifted through our midst the fantastic army of Flower People, now already turned into ghosts. So quickly does time run on, their passionate confronting of public brutality with public gentleness now seems almost totally unreal. The savage alignments of those days had about them such a relieving simplicity. I am aware that to many people in England the excesses of the Peace Movement occasioned feelings of near-amusement: but then near-amusement of this kind is one of the more obvious symptoms of an English strangeness.

As a foreigner in America, I became too possessed by the fever of that time, and the baffling contradictions it set off in my head. Obsessively I wanted to set out on paper the conflicting ideas which sprang up everywhere I looked – often enough taking the form of elaborate interior duologues. Over and over I returned to the apparent truth that an absolute non-aggressive position seems unattainable by Man without tangible loss of warmth and cherishable humanity – (what warm man will spare the Ruffian With the Pistol threatening his beloved?) – and yet a

113

S.—A*

relative, 'human' attitude which permits retaliating under extreme provocation inescapably leads to horrors unenvisaged and unintended at the start of it: witness Hiroshima as the end of the Second World War.

Man squeezed like a nut between an ideal choice and a practical one, and cracked in bits by either, is scarcely a novel image: yet the discovering of it for oneself, the coming to any sort of awareness of tragic ambiguity, must always be new and painful. I remember how angry I felt with my many opposed thoughts, and yet how also exciting I found the idea of Insoluble Situation. Walking around Manhattan, I was accompanied everywhere by the nagging exhilaration of irresolveable argument. As I contemplated the pop-eyed King of Sassania in the Metropolitan Museum, Mark Askelon contemplated him too over my shoulder, and voiced his mocking comments in my ear. (Mark himself, of course, has clear 'American' ancestors: brilliant Ezra Pound, or magnificent Orson Welles, living half-fulfilled and half-wasted by the Mediterannean Sea.) The actual figure of the young student with hair torn out of his head appeared to me suddenly one evening in the apartment of a friend, a few hours after a savage clash had occurred near Wall Street between a band of youngsters and a gang of construction workers. I can still see vividly the patch of white on his head.

I remember starting *The Battle of Shrivings* high up in a tiny work-room in the roof of the Dakota Building on West Seventy Second Street. For relief, I would walk out and breathe fresh air on a small gargoyle-bordered terrace overlooking glorious Central Park. If it has ever energised you at all, it is impossible to resist the anguish of this most urgent and beautiful of cities. Over me its spell has long been unbreakable. In those days of early work on the play, its concerns seemed to me so immense that flying from Kennedy to Heathrow Airport felt like flying out of the twentieth century back to the nineteenth. A truly multi-racial society would be receeding, in all the torment of its birth: approaching would be one chiefly insular, condescending, and frigid. This impression was of course unfair, and confessing it makes one seem self-righteous, but I was never happy in swinging, satirical London: the constant drizzle of put-down and small-minded preoccupation tended to dampen my spirits far too often.

I recall this feeling now because only now do I realise how living so much out of the country at that time enabled me to become infected with the need to discuss on stage, with flourish and head-on explicitness, the idea of human improvability. English dramatic taste rather deplores the large theme, largely broached: it tends to prefer – sometimes with good sense, but often with a really dangerous fear of grossness – the minute fragment, minutely observed. I am not saying that I did the job (or have re-done it) well. I simply reflect that had I remained a constant Londoner during that period, I doubt if I would have done it at all.

This said, I must confess that this second version of the play – composed three years ago, and now simply called *Shrivings* as earnest of plain intent – is much nearer to my original goal than was the first. I would like to thank my publisher deeply for letting me see it in print, laid out between hard and handsome covers, even though not interred in public acclaim. It is, after all, a brave act for a man of business to bring out a play which has yet to be produced on the stage. May the Protective God of Dramatists rain benefits upon him! And may the play itself now give me at last some kind of peace.

P.S.

THE SET

In the Middle Ages, Shrivings was a House of Retreat. Now it shows a wide, austere, light-filled interior of white-washed wall and crude timber, divided into two levels.

BELOW: the main living area of the house.

Two huge arches, left and right. That to the left frames the door to Gideon's study; that to the right frames the staircase. Between them, the room goes back under the lip of Mark's bedroom, to the back wall of the house, which contains a window. The front door is assumed to be off-stage right, in this same wall.

Two doors, downstage, left and right. That to the left leads to the garden; that to the right, to the kitchen.

Two tables, left and right. That to the left—standing diagonally to the audience—serves as a desk: a chair, behind it; two stools before it, a telephone on it and a pile of letters, half opened. That to the right, a long refectory table for dining: a bench on the upstage side of it.

All the furniture has been made by DAVID, which gives to the place an original look: cool, and beautiful.

At the head of the stairs, one can either turn right, to the other bedrooms, or left to MARK'S.

ABOVE: this room hangs over the playing area below, framed by the top half of the two large arches. It contains a bed and a table. Its window is assumed to be out front. The bathroom is off, to the left.

The whole atmosphere of this place is one of tranquillity and dedication.

CHARACTERS

GIDEON PETRIE:
Philosopher and President of the World League of Peace.

LOIS NEAL:
his secretary.

MARK ASKELON:
Poet and former pupil of Gideon.

DAVID ASKELON:
his son.

The action takes place at Shrivings, the
Cotswold home of Sir Gideon Petrie.

TIME: 1970

ACT ONE

Scene One: Friday evening
Scene Two: Friday night

ACT TWO

Scene One: Saturday night
Scene Two: Sunday morning

ACT THREE

Sunday night

ACT ONE

1. Friday Evening

Five o'clock. David, a boy of nineteen, sits in the middle of the room, carving the leg of a small table, which is upside down on a sheet. He wears a frayed blue shirt and frayed blue jeans; his hair is long, and there are woodshavings in it. He concentrates very hard on the work.
The telephone rings. He pays no attention. Finally Lois comes in calmly, carrying a cup of tea. She is a pretty American girl of twenty-five; tidy, efficient, and cheerful. She too wears her hair long and is dressed informally.

LOIS : [*picking up the phone*] Sir Gideon Petrie's Secretary . . . No, I'm afraid he always spends this hour after tea completely alone. Beg pardon? Yes, sir; the vigil will go ahead exactly as announced. Sir Gideon will sit in Parliament Square from two o'clock till eight, tomorrow and Sunday. All who care to join him we welcome. Peace.
   She hangs up and sits at the table, opening the letters.
   Why didn't you answer the phone?
DAVID : It didn't sound interesting. It had that ring to it which said 'World Organisation.'
LOIS : It's one of the neurotic symptoms of our time, you know, an inability to live in the real world.
DAVID : And where's that?
LOIS : OK.
DAVID : No: where is it?
LOIS : [*pointing to the desk*] This is the real world, David.
DAVID : Letters?
LOIS : *These* letters, yes.
DAVID : This is the real world. Here.
   He throws up a handful of shavings over his head.
LOIS : Ha, ha, ha. [*She turns to the desk*].

123

DAVID: Hey!
LOIS: [*Impatiently*] What?
DAVID: Hey!
LOIS: Hay is for horses.
The phone rings. She answers it.
Sir Gideon Petrie's Secretary. Beg pardon? . . . No, sir, there
is no conflict in any way. The vigil ends on Sunday night.
The Award will take place on Monday morning. Sir Gideon
receives it for his twenty-fifth book '*Explorations*'—and Mr
Askelon to mark the appearance of his *Collected Poems* . . .
Well, I would have thought the award of a world-famous
prize to two world-famous figures was Human Interest
enough . . . No, I'm sorry. Shrivings is a place of quiet, and
we like to keep it that way. Peace.
She hangs up, gently.
DAVID: You're beautiful.
LOIS: Me?
DAVID: You're so firm. It's marvellous to be firm like that.
LOIS: It sounds awful. 'Firm' 's a disgusting word for a girl.
DAVID: It's great when applied to breasts. And even greater
when applied to moral outline. That's what you've got. Moral
outline.
LOIS: [*amused*] Yeah, well why don't you just tidy all that
away now, before your dad comes?
DAVID: Why? It creates an impression of industry, and dedi-
cation.
LOIS: It makes a grundgy impression.
DAVID: What a beautiful word!
LOIS: You know, I really can't believe I'm finally going to meet
him. The great Mark Askelon! Do you think I should tell him
I've been in love with him ever since I read *Wafers of Death*
in Doubleday's Bookshop, the first day I arrived in New
York?
DAVID: 'Grundgy!' That's perfect!
LOIS: He wrote about Catholicism like it was a disease. If my
dad read any one of those poems, they'd have to take him
straight to the hospital . . . What about your mother? She
must have hated them.

124

DAVID: I bet she just laughed.

LOIS: But she was a believer?

DAVID: Giulia laughed about everything.

LOIS: Why do you call her that?

DAVID: Why not?

LOIS: She was your mother.

DAVID: Once. Since then, Father immortalised her in poetry. Now she belongs wholly to Penguin Books.

LOIS: She must have been incredible. I mean, to make a great poet give up writing revolutionary poems, and do all his writing about love!

DAVID: That's bad?

LOIS: Of course not. It's just irrelevant. Do you realise that some parts of this world are actually getting poorer? When you're faced with a fact like that, people's sex lives come to look a bit trivial, don't they?

DAVID: Absolutely.

> *He tries to kiss her. She turns away very coolly, slits open another letter with great dexterity. David shrugs.*
>
> *The door opens. Sir Gideon Petrie comes in. He is a gentle, noble man of over sixty. One senses a great toughness, both of intellect and staying-power. His manners show a charm composed of clarity, courtesy, and gaiety of spirit.*
>
> *There is about him a sort of sparkling serenity: a delicate earnestness, through which one glimpses a deep and passionate involvement. He contemplates the youngsters lovingly.*

GIDEON: Peace, my fliers.

LOIS: Peace, Giddy.

DAVID: Peace, Giddy.

LOIS: You're out early. It's not six yet.

GIDEON: I'm too excited to settle. When I think he'll be here any time now! My goodness! [*To David*] Are you up to it?

DAVID: No.

GIDEON: Nor me. He sets such standards, your father. Everything has to be so memorable.

DAVID: Yes.

GIDEON: How's the afternoon post?

LOIS: I've laid them out. [*Indicating piles of letters*] Requests to speak. Requests to write.

GIDEON: [*sitting at the desk*] Yes, yes, yes to all requests today! I can't refuse anybody on the day Mark Askelon first comes to Shrivings! Do you think we did right in closing it this weekend? It's been bothering me.

LOIS: Why not? We've all got to be selfish sometimes.

GIDEON: Have we?

LOIS: You're too hard on yourself, Giddy!

GIDEON: You know, I haven't been working in there at all. Just lying on my bed, remembering him. Seeing him on his terrace in the sunshine. The Sage of Corfu, under his trellis of vines! Like a Roman pugilist gone to seed.

LOIS: You mean fat?

GIDEON: Of course.

LOIS: Oh, no!

GIDEON: He was always a mountain! A *sacred* mountain, of course. Everybody came from miles to sit round the foothills and listen!

    Lois laughs.

And what wonderful talk it was, my goodness!

LOIS: What kind?

GIDEON: Well, the last thing I remember him discussing— and it was all of eleven years ago, mind you—was whether the heart's blood the Furies dropped on Athens in the 'Oresteia' was really their menstrual fluid.

LOIS: [*a little shocked: trying not to show it*] Gee! Oh, my!

DAVID: He really put a spell on you, didn't he?

GIDEON: [*glancing through the letters and ticking some*] From the first day he became my student at Cambridge! You know, the summer we met we went for our first walking tour. Even then, he moved through the Mediterranean as if he owned it.

DAVID: Do you see Giulia there too, under the trellis?

GIDEON: Whenever I picture your mother, it's always in movement.

DAVID: Me, too. She used to dance me to sleep, like other mothers sing. She'd light a candle and I'd have to watch her

126

shadow on the wall. Up and down, up and down, till I went off.

GIDEON: How exquisite.

LOIS: D'you know the last thing *I'd* see at night when I was a kid? A beautiful plastic Jesus, like the ones they have in taxis to prevent crashes, only bigger. It had these great ruby tears on its face, and I'd have to pray to it before turning out the light: 'Dear Lord, make me a Good Catholic and a Good American. Amen!' We all have different backgrounds, I guess.

GIDEON: [*laughing*] And yours made you the fierce Falcon you are today!

LOIS: [*smiling*] Oh sure! [*Scooping up the letters*] I'll do these now. While I've got the energy. [*She looks fondly at Gideon*] You're looking just great, d'you know that?

GIDEON: I feel just great: thank you. So are you, I may say.

LOIS: Really?

GIDEON: Prettier each day.

LOIS: [*flattered*] Ha, ha, ha!

Smiling, she takes the letters into Gideon's study, shutting the door.

GIDEON: You know, you two are absolutely complementary. A Falcon and an Owl. She can give you the gifts of the day. You can give her the gifts of the night.

DAVID: Oh, Giddy!

GIDEON: What, my dear?

DAVID: I can't give anybody anything. Sometimes I think all the opposite things I feel should just cancel me out, and make me invisible. Like all colours make up white.

GIDEON: You know, your father's going to be very impressed with you.

DAVID: Why not? I'm very impressive. It's not everyone who can drop out of two public schools, and Cambridge University, all in the space of five years.

GIDEON: Do you think Mark cares a fig about academic conformity?

DAVID: I don't know. I don't even know what he feels about me being here.

GIDEON: If *I* had a son, there's nowhere in the world I'd rather think of him than in your father's villa.

DAVID: Six years' silence, punctuated by telegrams. 'Regret still not convenient you return. Father.'

GIDEON: We've talked about this a great deal, my dear. Perhaps he did not feel able to write. It happens.

DAVID: And why does he come now? Certainly not just to get a prize. He's had hundreds offered, and never accepted one.

GIDEON: Perhaps he needs us. Have you thought of that?

DAVID: [*startled*] Needs?

GIDEON: Yes.

Suddenly David shudders violently.

David! What's the matter?

DAVID: Nothing.

GIDEON: But there is. Tell me.

DAVID: Nothing. Why do you listen to me? It's all nonsense!

GIDEON: Listen to me, then. Life hasn't been so easy for him these past years. People say hard things of him, I know. How heartless to forbid you the house all the time your mother was so ill. Was it so heartless to want to spare you the horror of watching her go? The paralysis claiming more of her each day?

DAVID: And afterwards? Staying there quite alone?

GIDEON: Your mother's death was the end of a world for Mark. I wonder if even you can quite conceive the end of a world. ... [*Warmly*] My dear, let's offer him this house these few days to be his home. Let's offer him Shrivings, with all its tradition of Peace. What d'you say? Oh my goodness: isn't that lovely work?

DAVID: Your goodness. [*Abruptly*] I'll take this back to the stables.

He picks up the table.

GIDEON: What are you trying to tell me?

Pause. Then the boy shrugs. Lois comes in.

LOIS: I've just typed the two for your personal signature.

GIDEON: I'll sign them.

With a look at David, Gideon retires to his study.

LOIS: [*tidying up*] Dinner's at eight. I've decided to make

Roman eggs in honour of your father. Do you think he'll appreciate the subtle compliment?

DAVID: I don't know.

He goes out into the garden with the unfinished table. She looks after him, puzzled, then sits at the desk and starts sorting out some more papers.

Pause. A voice is heard calling wooingly.

MARK: [*off*] Gideon! . . . Gideon! . . .

Lois looks up. Mark appears from the back, carrying a large package done up in sacking and a small parcel in brown paper. In his early fifties, he is the relic of an enormous man. A mass of hair falls from a massive head: eyes stare from an eroded face. He wears a Greek shepherd's cloak with a hood. His voice is still powerful.

LOIS: Peace.

MARK: What?

LOIS: Peace.

MARK: If possible.

He moves into the room, looking about him.

Stupendous!

LOIS: Can I help you?

MARK: Is that Lyssop Ridge up there behind the house?

LOIS: I'm afraid I don't know.

MARK: Those woods lie on it like a silver fox on a nigger's shoulder.

LOIS: [*offended*] May I ask who you are, please?

MARK: A shepherd, as my cloak proclaims. I suspect permanently without a flock. The name is Mark.

LOIS: [*amazed*] Not Mark *Askelon*!

MARK: Exactly so.

LOIS: How did you get here?

MARK: A hired Humber car in leatherette. It's just gone away.

LOIS: [*excited and suddenly nervous*] Oh Gee! I didn't expect you to . . . well to . . . look exactly like that! I didn't know what you'd look like really! . . . Where's your luggage?

MARK: In the hall. The maid can fetch it in later.

LOIS: We have no maids at Shrivings, sir. Sir Gideon does not approve of servants. Here everybody has to do his own room.

129

I do this and the kitchen. Of course you won't have to — —
I'll do yours, of course!

MARK: How many people stay here, then?

LOIS: Oh, it's just like a hotel. We've got fifteen bedrooms,
and we hope they'll be all filled every night. They're mostly
kids on their way someplace. We try not to turn anyone away
who genuinely wants a place to sleep.

MARK: You mean it's a sort of Commune for Transients?

LOIS: [laughing] Oh now, don't get scared! There's no one
coming this weekend. Giddy asked me to accept nobody for
the three days you're here. He figured you'd like some quiet.

MARK: And you do all the supervising?

LOIS: Sure! Giddy calls me a general factota! . . . My actual
name's Lois. Lois Neal . . . I'll get your case.

She runs off, and returns with a battered suitcase.

MARK: Where did he find you?

LOIS: [proudly] In jail, after a march! Two years ago. We
talked all night. In the morning he asked me to work for him.
I was terribly proud. I could type some, but I didn't know
any shorthand at all. So I took one of those Courses in
Speedwriting for With-It Girls. Do you know, after four
weeks I could do a hundred words a minute?

MARK: But surely there was a secretary here already?

LOIS: Oh, there was a grundgy old woman called Miss
Crawford. She looked like one of those Feminists from the
1910s. You know—white cuffs, and tits like dried apples. She
was going to retire anyway. One look at me, and she fled.

MARK: I bet she did.

LOIS: I think Giddy was glad to see her go—but of course he'd
never say.

MARK: You admire him very much, don't you?

LOIS: He's a saint. [Pause] Well, let me show you your room.

She turns and picks up the package wrapped in sacking.

MARK: [with a hint of sharpness] Please — let me carry that.

LOIS: [pleasantly] OK!

*She picks up the case instead, and goes upstairs. Mark
follows, leaving the small parcel behind on the table. They
enter the bedroom above.*

In here.

MARK: Thank you.

He puts his package on the table, down front.

LOIS: It's nice, isn't it?

MARK: Excellent.

He takes off his cloak. Underneath he is wearing a baggy old suit and a cheap cotton shirt.

LOIS: The bathroom's through there. I hope you like lemon soap. I put in a great cake of it.

He throws his cloak on the bed.

MARK: What's a saint?

LOIS: A man who doesn't know what it is to reject people.

MARK: And that's Gideon?

LOIS: He has no hostility left in him for anyone in the world.

MARK: Do you really believe that?

LOIS: Absolutely. He's proved it can be done.

MARK: You have American eyes.

LOIS: Is that good?

MARK: Eyes are inherited. Who gave you yours?

LOIS: I don't know. My father, I guess. He's a doctor in Chicago.

MARK: Does he approve your working for the President of The World League of Peace?

LOIS: God, no! All he thinks about is how to get me home, away from the enemies of the American way of life! . . . [*Gleefully*] Oh, gee, it's so great you're here! I'm making a special dinner in your honour. We're vegetarian here, you know.

MARK: We?

LOIS: Well, it's me really, I'm afraid. I'm a health food nut. Since I've come, Shrivings does without meat. Giddy entirely endorses this, I may say. I hope you don't mind. It's much better for you . . . I'm going to try and make a cream cheese soufflé for desert. It can be spectacular, but it's a bastard to get right.

MARK: You do all the cooking here?

LOIS: Sure. I enjoy it.

MARK: Yes, but do the diners?

LOIS: [*laughing*] Well, they say they do!

Gideon comes out of the study, and walks to the foot of the stairs.

Giddy says I should publish my recipes altogether and call it The Protester's Cookbook. I think that sounds just a little pompous, don't you?

GIDEON: [*calling upstairs*] Mark?

Mark comes out of the room. He looks down the stairs, and sees Gideon. He descends.

MARK: Gideon.

They embrace, very warmly.

GIDEON: My dear, you look marvellous!

MARK: [*coming into the living room*] You mean slimmer? It's true. God knows how, with my alcoholic constitution. Behold! [*He swirls across the room*] Man is a reed—but a drinking reed!

Gideon laughs delightedly. Lois comes down also.

As for you—you haven't changed a hair. Not one hair since last I saw you—eleven years ago, in Corfu harbour!

GIDEON: I wish that were true. Alas, my dear, at my age the last hairs fall even quicker than the last illusions. You've met Miss Neal, I see. More than a secretary—she's a conscience.

LOIS: Nonsense, Giddy!

MARK: Oh, I sensed that right away. My moral hazel twig pointed straight at her!

GIDEON: [*embarrassed for Lois*] You had a good flight, I hope?

MARK: Did I? We annihilated the Appenines, the Alps and the Dordogne in less than three hours. Is that good? . . . No matter. This room is compensation for anything!

GIDEON: It used to be a House of Retreat, you know.

MARK: Of confession, surely? Is that not what Shriving means? Confession and penance?

GIDEON: Oh well, I hope it won't be found too inappropriate for a thorough-going atheist.

MARK: I daresay a thorough-going rationalist has exorcised its spirit not a little.

They bow to each other.

Coming up your drive is an unforgettable experience. That long tunnel of elm trees, and at the end a great stone porch shouting Stop!

GIDEON: Shouting 'Come!' my dear. 'Come.'

MARK: Is it?

Slight pause. Then abruptly indicating the parcel:
Please open that. My present to your house.

GIDEON: My goodness! Whatever can it be?

MARK: [*to Lois*] Do you have wine?

LOIS: I've got a little for cooking. It's not very good, I guess.

MARK: So much the better. Household gods cherish the ordinary.

LOIS: [*admiringly*] Out of sight!

MARK: Please fetch it.

LOIS: Right!

She darts out to the kitchen. Gideon lifts from the smaller package an ancient Greek drinking cup of clay.

GIDEON: Oh, my dear! How exquisite!

MARK: A libation cup from the sixth century Before Cant!

GIDEON: I'm overwhelmed.

MARK: Wine was poured into that to toast the Gods.

GIDEON: I'm afraid it's been years since I drank wine.

MARK: What do you need with it? Your spirit is the last of the wine. After you, all is vinegar! . . . I shall put that into my speech about you.

GIDEON: Speech?

MARK: At the Prize Giving. I assume you are preparing one about me.

GIDEON: No. Surely that isn't part of the ceremony, that we eulogize each other?

MARK: If it isn't, I shall make it so.

GIDEON: Oh my goodness, I hope not!

Lois returns with an open wine bottle.

LOIS: Here!

MARK: Splendid! Giddy, you pour. [*Extending the cup*] Fill it to the brim.

GIDEON: Very well, my dear. [*He takes the bottle*] I can always rely on you to make a delicious ceremony out of everything!

133

[He pours the wine into the cup].
MARK: There now. Thank you . . . Attention, Please! *[He raises the cup]* I lift this cup of many consecrations! I drink to your house!
LOIS: Wow!
MARK: To Shrivings – in whose cool chambers the dangling soul was once tied to the trellis of confession, and so helped to flower.
David comes in from the garden, carrying a great object wrapped in a white sheet.
Here was sheath in a time of swords! Silence in a time of muskets! And now, in a time of bombs –
DAVID: Peace.
All look at him. A pause. He sets the object down. Then abruptly, Mark turns away and thrusts the cup at Gideon.
MARK: Complete the toast.
GIDEON: I couldn't, my dear. I'm afraid it would make my head swim.
MARK: You must – or there will be perturbation in the house.
DAVID: I'll drink for him.
Mark contemplates him, then hands him the cup. David drinks, wincing.
LOIS: I guess it's been open a few days.
MARK: Haven't we all? Well, not him perhaps . . . Well, I did not expect to see you so soon. It's charming of you to come all this way over from Cambridge.
DAVID: *[avoiding his eyes]* I . . . live here.
MARK: Live?
DAVID: I wrote to you.
MARK: I don't read letters.
DAVID: *[embarrassed]* I gave up Cambridge. And then Giddy – Gideon – suggested I move in here. So I did. I've been here since November.
MARK: You gave up?
DAVID: Well, it would have given me up. I just got in first . . .
GIDEON: Philosophy is not David's metier. He prefers at the

moment to make furniture for philosophers. A decision I selfishly encourage.

MARK: I don't understand.

GIDEON: All the furniture in this room was made by David. *Pause. Mark looks about him. He has difficulty in digesting this news.*

MARK: Extraordinary. Where did you learn?

DAVID: [*darting glances at his father, but unable to look him fully in the face*] I took woodwork at my last school. Then Giddy has an old stables here. I felt I wanted . . .

MARK: What?

DAVID: To do something with my hands.

MARK: Well, why not? . . . It's a noble profession, carpentry. The only one with an indisputable patron saint!

David laughs.

What's that you've got there? Something for my arrival?

GIDEON: [*confidently to Mark*] It's something special, I'm sure! He's been rather secretive lately. Are you going to show it to us!

DAVID: [*embarrassed*] Not now.

GIDEON: Of course now. Why ever not?

DAVID: Later. Tomorrow. I'll take it back. [*He moves to pick the object up again*].

GIDEON: [*in great surprise*] David! . . . Please show us. We're all dying of curiosity.

David stands staring at the ground.

LOIS: Come on, David, don't be so dopey!

He still stands not replying.

O.K. – *I'll* do it!

DAVID: No! [*To Gideon*] You! (*He smiles at Gideon*).

GIDEON: [*smiling back, intimately*] Me? I'm honoured.

Gideon approaches the object.

Hey presto! One – two – three!

He takes off the sheet. Underneath stands a throne of marvellous austerity. A pause.

GIDEON: How beautiful! Oh, how beautiful, David! It's the most lovely thing you've done yet.

DAVID: [*pleased*] Really?

135

LOIS: Wow!
DAVID: [*eagerly to her*] D'you like it?
LOIS: It's out of sight!... Honest!
GIDEON: What do you say, Mark? Isn't it fine?
MARK: I say felicitations to my son on his sense of things. He obviously sees what is lacking here. A true Cathedral needs a true Cathe*dra*!
LOIS: Cathedral?
MARK: That's where we are, isn't it? Shrivings, the Cathedral of Humanism.
GIDEON: Don't be naughty, Mark!
MARK: [*to David*] I'm right, aren't I? It is a throne?
DAVID: [*low*] Yes.
MARK: And for Giddy?
DAVID: Yes.
MARK: [*to Gideon*] Exactly so! All for *you*! The Chair of Paternal Wisdom. I would hope to earn one myself in time. Such objects have to be earned, eh, David?
    David shrugs haplessly.
GIDEON: You sit on it. It would become you far better, a throne.
MARK: Maybe–but it hasn't been offered! We're here to witness *your* coronation. So please get up there and sit down as impressively as you can manage!
GIDEON: [*grimacing modestly*] Very well. Thank you, David. [*He sits on the throne*].
    Mark claps.
MARK: Hail, Gideon! First Pope of Reason! Hail!
GIDEON: [*embarrassed*] Stop it now, Mark, really!
LOIS: Hail, Giddy! Hail, Giddy! Hail, Giddy!
GIDEON: Now, please! Really! Really!
LOIS: You look absolutely wonderful there! Doesn't he, Mr Askelon?
MARK: Exactly in place!
GIDEON: Perhaps I should take it with me on the vigil. Set it up in Parliament Square. It would evoke irreverent comparisons with the one in Westminster Abbey!
MARK: Vigil? What vigil?

136

LOIS: We're all sitting, tomorrow and Sunday afternoons.
MARK: [*alarmed*] You mean a demonstration?
LOIS: Yes. It's been in all the papers!
MARK: I don't read newspapers. In the end, that is the only truly obscene four-letter word: NEWS!
LOIS: We're hoping for at least ten thousand people. Why don't you come too? It'd be the most tremendous help to the Cause!
GIDEON: She's right. I'm known as a crank – but you would really be a catch.
MARK: Oh no, I don't think so.
LOIS: Oh why not, Mr Askelon? It would be so *great* having you!
MARK: [*lightly*] Let's say, I hate to be old-fashioned.
LOIS: [*bewildered*] Old-fashioned?
MARK: Peaceful protest is absolutely Out, my dear. The really modern young have quite abandoned vigils. Especially in your fair country.
GIDEON: Which is why she left it, Mark: for the moment. Until there's another real peace movement, and not just Young Violence joining with Old.
LOIS: Which will be never.
GIDEON: Oh, come now. All revolutionaries idealise their Movement's early days. Don't fall into the same trap. The Flower Children shouted some simple truths. Home has to be found: it's not the place you're born in. Country can be a mental prison, and patriotism an ape's adrenalin. Do you think that'll be forgotten?
LOIS: [*warmly*] Not when you speak, no!
MARK: [*Ironic*] And what did the flowers shout?
LOIS: Beg pardon?
MARK: If those daffodils could speak, which the flower boys handed out to policemen – if they could tell about their birth, through layers of icy spring soil, d'you know what they'd say? They'd open their yellow mouths and yell Violence! Violence! at the top of their stalks.
LOIS: [*laughing*] No, they would not! They'd shout Effort! That's not the same thing at all.

GIDEON: Well said, Lois!

MARK: *Touché!* . . . What would I have to do at your vigil? Sit in front of the House of Commons and chant Down With The Bomb!?

LOIS: We're concerned to ban all weapons, you know. Not just the bomb.

MARK: [*playfully*] Even penknives?

LOIS: Beg pardon?

MARK: Even vegetable knives? Those clever little knives which dice carrots for your joy-giving, life-enchanting salads?

LOIS: Well, that would be a dreadful idea!

MARK: What is not a weapon? The tongue, Miss Neal, can be a dreadful weapon. Should we have them all cut out?

LOIS: [*becoming a little confused*] I mean, here at Shrivings we think it is wrong to fight in any circumstances.

MARK: Any whatever?

LOIS: Any whatever!

She looks at Gideon for approval.

MARK: Even Hitler?

LOIS: Well, it is hard to adjust to that particular concept, I admit. But once you start fighting, you become as guilty as your enemy.

MARK: [*blandly*] You mean, the men who freed Belsen were as guilty as the men who made it?

LOIS: No, of course not.

MARK: Then what? The evil you don't fight, you enlarge.

GIDEON: [*softly*] No, my dear. The evil you do fight you enlarge. That's surely the point. You arm yourself to destroy gas chambers in Poland. Five years later, you are melting the eyeballs of fishermen on the Yellow Sea. We've had centuries of fighting back for Freedom and Justice. It doesn't work. We've had centuries of trying to *limit* fighting back: battle by mercenaries; truces on Christmas Eve. It doesn't work either. So long as boys can continue to hose each other down with fire on Boxing Day, their Christmas Day truce is an obscenity; a sop to the unseeing.

Pause. Reassuringly he squeezes Lois' hand.

MARK: [*brusquely*] If a ruffian with a pistol entered this room, and was definitely going to kill Miss Neal – assuming you had a pistol too, would you use it on him?

GIDEON: No.

MARK: You would let him kill her?

GIDEON: I have no choice, unless I wish to become him.

MARK: [to Lois] Same situation. Would you let him kill Giddy?

LOIS: Yes.

MARK: Touching loyalty you have for each other here at Shrivings!

LOIS: We do!

MARK: Apparently.

LOIS: Shrivings is the loyalty!

MARK: [to David] What would you do, my son?

Pause.

DAVID: Is it a girl ruffian or a man?

LOIS: What difference does *that* make?

DAVID: I think I'd use the gun.

MARK: Why?

DAVID: Because I'd rather have Lois alive than somebody I didn't know.

MARK: Unreasonable boy! And she's not even flattered, are you?

LOIS: [to David] How can you be so subjective about everything? It's like you can't grasp the simplest general idea!

MARK: Don't blame him too harshly, Miss Neal. Beauty, after all, confuses the best of us!

LOIS: [embarrassed] Oh! Well! Gee! . . .

MARK: I must confess that I myself, seeing you threatened by this ruffian, would have a hard time leaving you to your fate.

LOIS: Thank you!

MARK: But I would, of course. Out of deference to your principles.

LOIS: [nervously] Oh, of course!

MARK: [his tone darkening] I would – with the utmost regret – abandon you to his pistol. Or to his razor. Or to the dungeons of the Inquisition. Or the locomotives of Chiang Kai-Chek, who, I have been told, fed his prisoners into their furnaces in

139

S.—B

order to keep them running. Or for that matter, to the hands of New York Construction workers . . . [*He stops suddenly*].

GIDEON: [*puzzled*] Mark?

MARK: [*his tone totally changed*] Have you seen the Ruffian at work? Really seen him? Have you, Giddy? You sit here so calmly . . . Have you seen a boy scalped? I have. Last year – in the civilised city of Manhattan . . . [*Pause*] I'd gone there after Giulia died, to keep busy, as they say.

GIDEON: Yes, I heard that you went.

MARK: To declaim poems to college students, written twenty years before they were born . . . They were in fact swarming all over the city the day I arrived: yet again protesting the Vietnam War – in this instance, the invasion of Cambodia. Isn't it amazing the way the Young simply won't give up? There they all were, in their velvets and zippy boots – haircuts like so many liberty bells – still handing out pamphlets, still squeaking 'Stop Killing' in desperate little voices. And the next day their elders – as if the murder of four children in Ohio that week had not been enough – decided to punish their impertinence in New York. [*Pause*] I was sitting with my lawyer in his office in Wall Street. Suddenly we heard this roar outside – it was about noon: a sort of sea of approaching fury. We walked to the window. Four floors below us, a terrified group of youngsters was standing quite still. On both sides of them stood massed ranks of workers from the building trade – men whose present affluence has apparently compelled them into the right wing. Dreadful-looking thugs, with faces like huge steaks, wearing hard yellow hats. And then we watched *their* protest: *their* statement of human dignity. For fifteen minutes, they beat the children into pulp. They bashed them with their fists. They kicked them in the balls and the breasts with steel toes. They tore cheeks from faces. They danced on vomitting girls. And then they swept on, shouting 'America! America!' – round the corner, to the next gang-bang. And all the while, not moving, not doing anything stood policemen, – their Irish potato faces barely concealing smiles. [*Pause*] My lawyer, a fellow of infinite social conscience, had dashed into the street, leaving me alone. Suddenly the place was quiet again, and there was only one figure visible. A boy, sitting on the kerb, wearing a sort of eiderdown. Lumps of hair had been torn from his head. Can you imagine the force that needed? – and he was moaning in unspeakable pain. But with some kind of instinct for city tidiness, he was carefully dropping what blood he could into a drain. I stood in the window watching him, a dry martini in my hand. It was a day of April. Clouds of pollen were streaming down the street between us. Golden dust tumbling through the air. It seemed to be settling over him, like dandruff . . . And then he raised his head and looked at me.

LOIS: What did you do?

MARK: [*brutally*] I raised my glass.

LOIS: [*confused*] But . . . but couldn't you have? –

MARK: What?

LOIS: Well, gotten him an ambulance?

MARK: I could. But I wanted another drink.

A shocked pause.

Abruptly he goes upstairs into his bedroom, and bangs the door. Gideon moves after him, but suddenly the door is loudly locked from the inside. Mark sits on the bed, his face in his hands.

LOIS: He's nuts! He's completely *nuts*!

GIDEON: Lois, please.

LOIS: What's that supposed to mean? What's he *talking* about?

GIDEON: He was always addicted to drama. You know that.

LOIS: Drama?

GIDEON: Why don't you just start dinner?

LOIS: Jesus! . . . [*regaining control*] OK!

She goes out to the kitchen. David stands unmoving, staring at the stairs.

GIDEON: It's just fatigue. That's all. He'll be down for dinner . . . Why don't we take a walk in the garden? What do you say? . . . *David* . . . He's simply tired –

David turns and goes abruptly into the garden. Puzzled, Gideon follows him. Above, Mark springs up from the bed. He opens his case and takes out two bottles of brandy, which he places on the shelf. Then he returns and extracts another two, which he also puts on the shelf. Then he takes out one shirt, closes the case, and kicks it under the bed. He turns to the package in its sacking on the table. He places his hands on it.

MARK: Proteggimi. Proteggimi. Proteggimi! . . . And him. Keep him safe from me. By your limbs, I beg you. By your murdered limbs, keep them all out of harm from me: Gideon – David our son – that silly girl.

He unties the string and stuffs it into his pocket. Then he lowers the sacking to reveal a black wooden box with doors. On the top is a little pediment in pink wood: this he erects, with a deliberate delicacy.

My wife. My own true wife. Santissima, Beatissima Giulia!

Standing behind it, he opens the doors of the box to reveal, staring straight at us, the head in effigy of a young woman painted in naive style. The whole shrine is coloured in the gay, crude manner of peasant work from Southern Italy: on the inside flaps of the doors are bright, little gilded saints. Mark moves round and kneels to it, reverently.

MARK: I'll not go down there again. I'll keep in here till the prize-giving. Then straight back to Corfu – hurting no one. I swear it, my darling. Te lo juro! Te lo juro, mia moglie! *Santa Giulia Paralytica!*

SLOW BLACK OUT

2. Friday Night

Ten-thirty. As the lights come up, Lois is clearing the dinner table. David sits cross-legged on the floor, rolling a joint. Upstairs, Mark lies on his bed. One hand holds a half-empty bottle.

DAVID: I saw an armoured car today.

LOIS: What?

DAVID: In Trister village, just before dinner. Well, it was one of those converted ones. At first I thought it was full of chrysanthemums. Then just as they passed me, they all separated, and turned out to be four shaggy male heads and four shaggy female, all the same colour bronze. If I'd chosen the next street, there'd have been no car. If I'd seen them at the next corner, they'd already have separated.

LOIS: Are you stoned?

He does not reply.

She gives him a bewildered face, and goes into the kitchen with her tray. David lights his joint. Mark stirs on the bed.

MARK: Brilliant. Absolutely brilliant! Not ten minutes in the house, go off like that – bang! Just for one pretentious American slit . . . [He sits up and looks at the shrine] No, it was his fault, the boy. Coming in like that – your eyes in his head! . . . Who knew he was here? . . . Standing there like some medieval half-wit, all shrugs and shavings in the hair. Who the hell is he? Master carpenter to Gideon Petrie. I sent him to England for *that*? – to carve his throne! 'Hail to my new daddy, – Lord of the twenty-five books!' My old daddy only wrote four, and they were just poetry! That doesn't count . . .

Lois returns with a bowl containing four green apples. She piles the remaining plates on the tray. David watches her.

MARK: And what about his eyes, eh? Gideon's? Did you see all that white gum in the corners? My God, he's aged!
He lifts the bottle to his lips, and drinks.
DAVID: Smash one.
LOIS: Huh?
DAVID: Say Let this Plate be Dad, and smash it. Banish the Demon Uptight.
LOIS: It wouldn't.
She goes on piling the plates.
MARK: [*half to himself*] 'Peace!' 'Peace!' What's that supposed to mean? Well, of course, you could hear it – – defiance. 'I'm Giddy's boy now. Let's not mistake . . . Son and heir of Shrivings . . .' Sagging Jesus!
DAVID: [*warmly*] I'm sorry.
LOIS: I mean, OK, I just wish you'd warned me in advance. I wish you'd told me; please overlook my Dad's behaviour, because he's clinically insane. I'd have been prepared.
DAVID: He's not.
LOIS: Yeah, well, like what's he doing up there now, locked in his room all night? No dinner – nothing.
DAVID: Your elbows are very upset.
LOIS: What?
DAVID: They're up in arms.
LOIS: Ha, ha, ha. [*She picks up the full tray*].
DAVID: Hey.
LOIS: Hay is for horses. [*She goes into the kitchen*].
MARK: [*to the shrine*] Alright, dance for him. You dance for him. [*He gets off the bed, and stands glaring at the shrine*] You go in there and dance him to sleep *now*! Try it, why don't you? Get out of bed, and try it! . . .
He begins a drunk parody 'dance', singing to himself.
Sitting below, David looks upwards. The dance stops.
[*Shouting at the shrine*] Alright, stop it! Just stop . . . Sad looks. Reproach . . . Well, well! Can't you ever cry? Can't you ever fight me like a woman, not fucking saint? . . .
He starts pacing about. David rises anxiously to his feet.
That damn book. Always that prayer book! Can't you see it's disgusting? Filthy coloured pictures – Christ the Shepherdess!

144

Have you got no dignity at all, praying to a Bearded Lady?
Signora Gesù, Little Bo-Peep of Souls!
He starts to laugh – snatches up a large white towel, and lurches off to the bathroom.
Below, David shudders. Lois comes in with a cloth to wipe the table.
LOIS: What's the matter?
DAVID: [*not looking at her*] On the terrace.
LOIS: What?
DAVID: He'd sit and watch me for hours. Straw hat – eyes . . .
LOIS: What are you talking about?
DAVID: When I used to play . . . I'd go la-la-la, pretending to sing.
LOIS: I thought you adored him. You sort of said . . . [*He turns and shrugs, hopelessly*] Look, why don't you go up there now? It's obviously what he'd like.
DAVID: It isn't.
LOIS: Of course it is. It must be.
DAVID: It isn't.
LOIS: How do you know?
He shrugs again.
Well then what does he *want*?
DAVID: I'll whisper it. Here.
She approaches, puzzled. He kisses her abruptly. She lets herself be kissed, but remains inert.
Thank you.
LOIS: You're welcome.
DAVID: You know something? You're so uptight, it's a joke.
LOIS: A person is not uptight, my dear, just because she doesn't happen to want that.
DAVID: I think she is. I think that's exactly what she is.
LOIS: [*gently*] Or because she respects somebody else's opinions. I know it's me being pompous again. OK. But we've talked about this one hundred times. This is Giddy's place. His whole meaning. Don't you realise this is where he did it? Probably in this very room.
DAVID: [*Sarcastic*] Wow! . . .
LOIS: Do you think it was easy for a normal man to go to his

wife on his forty-fifth birthday and tell her he can't have sex anymore?

DAVID: It certainly wasn't easy for her, was it? She buggered off, and maybe that's exactly what I should do too.

LOIS: [*alarmed*] What d'you mean?

DAVID: Piss off, that's what I mean. Exit. Is that what you want? Come on, tell me. Is that what you'd like – for me to go, as she did?

LOIS: Don't be silly. You know I'd hate it.

DAVID: [*warmly*] Would you?

LOIS: I'm simply asking you to respect the spirit of a great man in his own house, that's all.

DAVID: [*playfully*] Because he's a vegetarian, we all have to be?

LOIS: Yes.

DAVID: Even though he doesn't mind?

LOIS: Yes. Because I do. On his behalf.

DAVID: You know what you are? You are a Disciple.

LOIS: And proud of it.

DAVID: I don't know a word that means so many boring things.

LOIS: OK: I'm boring. I know it. You're not saying anything new.

DAVID: I didn't mean that.

LOIS: It doesn't matter.

DAVID: I don't know what I mean. Not from one second to the next!

LOIS: If you could ever get involved, you might just find out. Till then you're like a sort of ghost, tapping on the window. Do you know?

He pulls 'ghost faces' at her.

I'm serious David. I mean it! . . . [*She breaks up laughing*] Oh cut it out!

She returns the faces. They are both playing, when Gideon comes out of his study.

GIDEON: I suppose Mark hasn't been down?

LOIS: No sign of him.

GIDEON: Then I'd better go up.

DAVID: D'you think you should?

GIDEON: We're starting a Vigil of Peace tomorrow. We can't leave distress at home . . . Are you coming with us?

LOIS: Of course he is! Oh, Giddy, it's going to be wild! I heard on the radio they're expecting twenty-five thousand people. Isn't that crazy? You'll have to address them.

GIDEON: Will I?

LOIS: Well, of course. The eyes of England will be upon you!

GIDEON: Oh, my goodness.

LOIS: You'll have to say something witty and profound.

DAVID: And very loud: the open air.

GIDEON: Very well. I shall say – 'Go home, the lot of you! What the devil do you think you're doing here, parading the streets in fancy dress, and annoying the police who have far more important things to do than take care of you lot!'

Both the youngsters laugh. Gideon ascends his throne with an air.

'What is it you want? We have educated you, at vast expense, in all the wisdom at our disposal. You've been given expert courses in all the right subjects. Mangerism, or worship of Family; Flaggism, or worship of Tribe; Thingism, or worship of Money. In our theatres and on our screens, we have taught you to find the act of killing men exciting, and the act of creating them obscene. You can go to Church, and respect the stopped mind. You can go to the war memorials, and respect the stopped body. What more do you want?'

Both youngsters laugh and clap.

LOIS: Oh, Giddy, that's great! You've got to say it – just like that!

GIDEON: And then, perhaps I'll ask them what they *really* want. If they are honest, they'll reply: 'A point to our lives. A meaning.' 'Very well, then,' I'll say: 'ask yourselves who you are. Look at each other. What do you see there? A crowd of weird beings, standing half-in, half-out of Nature. Animals possessed of powers completely non-animal. Powers to symbolise, to imagine, to laugh with self-ridicule. What could they be, these powers, if not tools to help free you from the violent, circular force which dominates all other life? [*He sits*]

147

Scientists go about the world looking for the Missing Link. It is staring them in the face. [*Pointing to David*] You are the Missing Link. [*Pointing to Lois*] You are the link between animals and what must appear if we are not to be sucked back into annihilation. Remember, as animals we are failures, and as aggressive beings also. We have to come at last to see Ego in a new way. As a pod, evolved for our protection during our years through pre-history, but which has now become our prison. If we are not to suffocate in it, we have to burst it open.'

LOIS: Wow!

GIDEON: We know more and more about our aggressions. We can't ever hope to remove them by reason alone: but if we don't make the attempt, not merely to concentrate their fury on to ever-lessening objects, but absolutely to starve them to death, we are doomed. Let me simplify it for you the point of a crazy imperative. The Drug Children of today cry: "Unite with Nature!" I say: Resist her. Spit out the anger in your daddy's sperm! The bile in your mother's milk! The more you starve out aggression, the more you will begin yourselves!'

DAVID: Oh, that's beautiful!

GIDEON: 'Fight your instinctive dislike of other people. Fight the clinging to possession. Fight the need to invent enemies. If you want fights, I have them for you in plenty! I tell you, you must fight all the preserving mechanisms which you have inherited from evolution. Only so can you fulfil your Destiny. I detest that word. It is fascist, and Siegfriedish and faintly embarrassing. But I can't think of another. Man *has* a Destiny: to be a loving creator, or a dead duck!' . . . How about that?

DAVID: [*laughing*] You're a mad old ham, aren't you?

LOIS: David!

GIDEON: Not too mad, I hope.

DAVID: I don't know.

GIDEON: Anyway, I've made a huge decision. I'm going to fast, all weekend!

LOIS: Fast? Whatever for?

GIDEON: [*getting up*] I've been thinking what his father was saying: how vigils and protests are out of date. Well, there's really nothing I can do about that, since war and violence are even more out of date. But the least I can do is pep things up a bit. Inject a little show business into proceedings! Hence the fast. If I were to faint from hunger on the pavement, the effect could be sensational.

DAVID: I don't like it.

GIDEON: Oh, come. Pathos still remains the best way of influencing the middle classes.

LOIS: I think it's out of sight! Why don't we ask everyone who comes to fast too?

DAVID: And pass out too, all at the same time! You could blow your nose as a signal, and twenty-five thousand people could collapse, holding their tummies.

LOIS: Ha, ha, ha!

GIDEON: No, she's got a good idea, David. [*To Lois*] Look, why don't you ring the newspapers? We can make the first editions if we hurry. Say I'm announcing a two day hunger protest and would like everyone who's coming tomorrow to stay hungry as well. The Press will love it. It's so delightfully vulgar.

LOIS: [*getting up*] Great!

GIDEON: They always say my head's in the clouds. They'll have to admit this is pretty nifty.

LOIS: I'll get started right away. And you two go to bed. You'll need your strength. Both of you, now. [*She goes out into the study*].

GIDEON: What's the matter?

> *Pause.*

DAVID: Starving people aren't protected.

GIDEON: [*puzzled*] Protected? Against what? . . . Why should I need protection?

> *Pause. David shrugs, looking at the floor.*

GIDEON: Are you being fanciful again? . . . I'll go and see your Father. You go to bed. Things will look fine in the morning.

> *He goes to the stairs. David rises anxiously. Gideon turns, aware of this.*

[*Amusedly*] I should think pot is allowed on a fast, wouldn't you? Does that make you any happier?
DAVID: Peace.
> *The boy walks rapidly past him, and runs upstairs, out of sight. To the right Gideon ascends after him. He knocks on Mark's door.*
GIDEON: Mark! . . . Mark!
> *Mark appears slowly from the bathroom.*
Let me see you, please. Just for a moment.
> *Mark moves into the room, without replying.*
I beg you. Please let me in.
> *Mark stands before the shrine.*
Mark . . .
MARK: [*whispering to the shrine*] Se viene, non ne sono responsabile!
GIDEON: I'll not go away till I've seen you. There. What do you think of that? I'll stay here all night. It'll be the start of my vigil.
> *Mark laughs aloud.*
Come on, now! Let me in! [*He rattles the door-handle*].
MARK: Non ne sono.
> *He moves to shut the doors of the shrine – then pauses and mischievously opens them again. Then he goes to the door, unlocks it and retreats to the bed, where he sits. Gideon enters.*
GIDEON: Peace.
MARK: I am surprised.
GIDEON: By what?
MARK: To find locks at Shrivings.
GIDEON: People require privacy at times.
MARK: [*sarcastically*] You mean for love-making?
GIDEON: [*imperturbably*] Among other things.
MARK: And who makes love here?
GIDEON: Youngsters stay every night. I imagine they're at it all the time.
MARK: How does Miss Neal regard that? Is she delighted by all that hippy coition?
GIDEON: [*smiling*] I think she tends to turn a blind eye.

MARK: Yes, I seen that blind eye. It's magnificent. A great improvement on your ex-wife's, to be honest.

GIDEON: Really?

MARK: Enid's eyes were like two pebbles in a January stream. I can say that now.

GIDEON: You've lost none of your naughtiness, my dear!

He turns and sees the shrine.

MARK: Giulia's of course, you remember. Around them flared that corona. Invisible there, of course. But quite detectable in David.

GIDEON: Yes.

MARK: I had her made by a craftsman in Corfu, from an old photograph. As a souvenir, she works well. Also as a reliquary.

GIDEON: Reliquary?

MARK: For her ashes.

Pause.

GIDEON: How beautiful.

MARK: Yes, well there we are. Two old men with two dead wives.

GIDEON: To be pedantic – you are still young, and Enid is still alive.

MARK: Married to an accountant I believe.

GIDEON: Yes. In Berkshire.

MARK: Isn't that death?

GIDEON: [*laughing*] You really are outrageous!

MARK: Do you miss her?

GIDEON: Very much.

MARK: Still?

GIDEON: Yes.

MARK: I leave tomorrow.

GIDEON: Leave?

MARK: For Corfu.

GIDEON: I won't hear of it. Why?

MARK: I'm out of practice at being a guest.

GIDEON: [*gently*] There are no guests at Shrivings. You're part of a family, and have to work at it.

MARK: Is my son part of this family?

GIDEON: Everybody is who stays here.

MARK: And he's stayed six months. He must enjoy it. Naturally. The more unreal the place, the more he would thrive.

GIDEON: Unreal?

MARK: We are not Place People, David or I. My father was not called Askelon, but Ashkenazy. Israel Ashkenazy, of the ghetto face. He bequeathed me no home on earth: only envy of home in others. That boy will never walk a Dorset lane like an Englishman – rock a Vermont porch like a Yankee – doze under a Corfu cypress like a Greek. He's a mongrel! Russo-Jewish-English-Neapolitan! Whelped in one island, weaned in another.

GIDEON: [with energy] Then lucky him! He at least has no chance to fool himself with illusion! We are all mongrels, Mark. Don't hunt for your home in the bloodstream! Home is an act of will.

MARK: Do you imagine?

GIDEON: Make no mistake: Shrivings is real. It would still be real if it were a tent or a set of shacks. Ask the people who come here, the hopeful young, who flood in every night. It's not a family, as so many people know it – a box of boredom for man and wife – a torture chamber for the children. That idea of family must soon be obsolete, surely? – a miserable little group, marked off by a flat door, or a garden fence! . . . [Ardently] No, my dear. Here is a new place of love. Stay with us, not just till Monday. See it for yourself . . . This one weekend, for your sake, I broke all rules and closed it – just to give us time alone. I believe I was wrong.

He extends his hand.

MARK: [coldly] I leave tomorrow. No more questions.

GIDEON: [very gently] We simply will not allow it.

MARK: Please go.

GIDEON: I can't believe you mean this.

MARK: Go!

Pause.

GIDEON: Peace.

Gideon leaves the room. Mark sits on for a moment, takes a swig from his bottle—then suddenly rushes downstairs after him. Startled, Gideon turns.

MARK [*blurting it out*] Alright! *Save me!*
>   *Pause.*
>   *Lois comes out of the study. Mark immediately turns away.*
LOIS: Oh, excuse me.
GIDEON: It's alright, my dear.
LOIS: I talked with six papers. They're all printing something in their first editions.
GIDEON: Good girl. [*He silently signs for her to go upstairs*].
LOIS: Don't stay up too late. Goodnight, Mr Askelon. [*Tenderly*] Peace.
>   *He nods. She goes upstairs. Pause.*
GIDEON: Save you from what?
MARK: Dust.
GIDEON: Dust?
MARK: Pollen.
GIDEON: That morning you spoke of. In New York. The riot in New York.
MARK: Yes?
GIDEON: There was pollen in the streets.
MARK: Yes.
GIDEON: Well? What of it?
MARK: It's hard.
GIDEON: Yes?
>   *A long pause.*
MARK: It was there between us. Me and that student. Between us in a long stream. I remained at my lawyer's window, looking down at him. He sat there on the kerb looking up at me, through that curtain of pollen. We lasted like that forever. I mean, five minutes. Five centuries in another sense, until I saw him transformed to an earlier time, five hundred years at least, when Wall Street was just a granite ledge padded by Redskin feet, and he another human sack, holding its scalped head . . . Five hundred years and no change. Five thousand, and still the identical horror. The tcarers and the torn. The orderers. The Penalisers. The Joyless, returning and returning like the spring – Unalterable . . . Do you know the taste of Unalterable? That boy sat glued to the earth,

with the pollen twirling round his red scalp – clouds of glinting dust – round and round the blood patch, like flies . . . I leant out, and it flew up to my mouth. I breathed it. I chewed it. – It entered my stomach like powdered drug: dead spring – round, dead, unalterable spring, with its meaningless glints of hope! On and on we glared at each other, and on and on his blood dripped into the drain, and the pollen twirled inside me, and the years turned, till I was sick. Till I vomited down the side of that smart new building. I saw my sick running down the glass walls, and the boy began to laugh.

GIDEON: Oh, my dear Mark! My poor man!

MARK: There he sat – blond puppet, in his eiderdown! There he sat on the kerb – my wife, in her canvas jacket, staring at me, those fixed eyes, 'Gesù! Gesù!'

GIDEON: Your wife?

MARK: Yes! . . . YES! . . .

Pause.

Public murder or private: it's all the same.

GIDEON: [*bewildered*] Murder?

MARK: Pull the hair out – pull the life. It's all the same. Takes longer, of course. Ten years longer. But it's all the same.

GIDEON: What do you mean, Mark? Murder?

MARK: [*drily*] Killing. Taking the life of.

GIDEON: What are you saying?

MARK: I'm saying I killed my wife. Is that hard to understand?

GIDEON: Oh, look – my dear . . .

MARK: Yes?

GIDEON: This is entirely my fault. I should never have left you alone in that villa! I should have come out myself and brought you back here. I ask you to forgive my selfishness . . . Sometimes one makes the most terrible mistakes: just for fear of intruding on grief.

MARK: Grief? Is that all you see, then? *Grief*?!

GIDEON: It is the most warping emotion in the world.

MARK: The great poet, grieving for his love! Sagging Jesus! . . . Look at you. What can you see? [*Viciously*] Gummy worried old eyes. What can you really see, Giddy, through all that white gum?

154

Pause.
GIDEON: [*imperturbably*] I like to think of it as spirit gum.
Pause.
MARK: [*lower*] Twelve years ago, you couldn't see. Even when you were in Corfu, I'd already started to kill her. You couldn't see it.
GIDEON: [*distressed*] My dear – my dear, dear man . . .
MARK: Even if I told you every detail. If I described to you exactly how I finished her off – what I actually *did* to her on her last night on earth . . . you wouldn't believe me. I'm your darling. Your first flier.
GIDEON: Of course you are.
MARK: Your eagle.
GIDEON: Yes.
MARK: No, Giddy.
GIDEON: [*passionately*] Yes, my eagle! The most marvellous pupil I ever had. The most marvellous friend!
MARK: [*quietly*] Stop it.
GIDEON: That's what you could never quite believe: that everything you did was a *marvel* to me.
MARK: Please stop it, Giddy.
GIDEON: Now I've found you again I'm not going to let you go until I've mended those damaged wings and sent you soaring up again into the sky of action – your proper element – your *real place*!
MARK: *Stop it! Will you stop it?*
Pause. He draws Gideon gently to him, and stares into his face.
[*Softly*] Believe me, old master, I could tear the faith out of your head, as easy as they tore the hair out of that boy.
GIDEON: [*levelly*] My goodness.
Gideon smiles. They remain unmoving, very close together, staring at each other.
MARK: Poor Mark. Grief has made him quite dotty, hasn't it?
GIDEON: A little unfair on himself, I think.
MARK: [*Quietly*] Is there no way of convincing you of your danger?
GIDEON: From you? . . .

155

MARK: [*intensely*] It isn't grief, Giddy! Be warned.

GIDEON: Then what, my dear?

MARK: The dust. It seeks converts . . . Do you know how long it took me to fall finally from your faith? The time it takes vomit to slide down a wall. Now I know – and have to make others know.

GIDEON: What do you know?

MARK: That the Gospel According to Saint Gideon is a lie. That we as men cannot alter for the better in any particular that matters. That we are totally and forever unimproveable.

GIDEON: No.

MARK: We will kill forever. We will persecute forever. We will break our lust forever on enemies we invent for the purpose.

GIDEON: No.

MARK: We are made of hostility as the spring is made of pollen. And each birth renews it, as the spring renews the year.

GIDEON: No.

MARK: Prove it.

GIDEON: Impossible. It is a faith, like others.

MARK: [*ironically*] Faith! Saint Gideon Petrie on his peacock throne of Reason, ringed by the irises of adolescence! Do you know what they say about you? Your discipline alone can save the world – because you alone have withered out of yourself entirely the roots of hate. Is it possible? [*Slyly*] How if I showed them their delusion – Miss Neal, and my doting son? . . . 'Stay with us,' you say, 'in this Commune of Love.' I say, if I chose, they would see you drive me out of it with hate.

GIDEON: Never.

MARK: Within one week.

GIDEON: Never.

MARK: Within one weekend.

GIDEON: [*serenely*] Never. Never. Never.

> *Pause.*

MARK: [*hard*] Very well. Let's see? . . . I propose a battle. It is now Friday night. I say by Monday morning – day of our joining award of Humane Letters – you will have thrown me out of Shrivings. How about that?

156

GIDEON: You would lose.

MARK: *I want to lose!* Because, if you lose, it'll be an end for both of us . . . If you can survive me with all your gentleness intact, I will stay here and work as your disciple. But you succumb – order me out of here, for whatever reason – and you will not again be able to preach Improveability. As for me, once you slam that door upon me, I will stagger down your tunnel of elm trees into the arms of Mother Church. Whether Roman or Greek to be later determined. So. I give you The Battle of Shrivings. *[He drinks]*.

GIDEON: You know, my dear, you really are the naughtiest man in the world!

MARK: Aren't I?

GIDEON: I think you'd say anything for the sake of drama!

MARK: I come out of the dust. Into the Church of Man. Do I joint it, or pull it down? . . . You're right. I'm ridiculous. Goodbye. *[He strides to the door]*.

GIDEON: Mark!

Mark pauses; turns.

Stay in this house as long as you wish. Shrivings will never reject you.

MARK: So be it.

GIDEON: Now it's very late. We can resume this tomorrow, surely?

MARK: You have no choice, now.

GIDEON: *[amused]* Oh my goodness.

Mark goes to the stairs, then turns.

MARK: Don't you know who I am?

GIDEON: Who?

MARK: The Ruffian with the pistol. Shoot me, and *you're* dead.

GIDEON: Peace, my friend.

MARK: Impossible. Battle has begun.

He goes upstairs. Gideon stares after him, then goes into his bedroom. The light fades.

CURTAIN

157

ACT TWO

1. Saturday Night

Eleven o'clock. Mark sits alone at the desk, listening to a large transistor radio.

BBC ANNOUNCER: In the debate which followed, Mr Lucas Brangwyn, the Member for Bloomsbury, called the wholesale destruction of Devonshire Square 'nothing less than a national scandal'. In his reply the Minister of Housing said nobody regretted the passing of old London more than he, but he sincerely believed the demolition had been carried out in what would ultimately be the best interests of the British public.

Pause.

This afternoon at two o'clock, Sir Gideon Petrie sat down in Parliament Square, Westminster, to begin the first of his two six-hour vigils outside the House of Commons in protest against the manufacture of all arms in the United Kingdom. He was accompanied by members of the World League of Peace, of which Sir Gideon is president: as well as many students and well-wishers. Minor outbreaks of violence occured when a group representing the League of Empire Loyalists threw bags of refuse over the sitting figures. They were moved on by the police.

Mark smiles.

Sir Gideon, who is also on a two-day fast, appeared composed and smiling throughout.

Pause.

The forecasters say that the easterly winds sweeping the country are dying down and it will become warmer tomorrow, but with a chance of showers –

Mark twiddles the dial. Loud rock music comes out of the radio. He turns it off contemptuously. The front door slams. Mark rises, hearing the voices of the returning

protesters. He tip-toes out into the kitchen. Into the room come Gideon, Lois and David, flushed and excited, taking off their thick outdoor clothes.
Chattering, they peel off scarves and boots. David relieves Gideon of his overcoat and beret, and hangs it up on the peg by the garden door.
LOIS: Yeah, that was great! *That* was the best!
DAVID: No, the old man in the top hat was the best!
LOIS: Yeah, but did you see the old woman in the fur coat dancing the Hare Krishna with those kids? I acted dumb, you know – pretending not to know, and I asked her what she was doing. Do you know what she said? [*Cockney accent*] 'I don't know, love. It's a new religion. Ride-a-Christian!'
GIDEON: [*laughing*] That's delightful! I wish I'd heard that.
LOIS: Isn't it great?
DAVID: D'you know who I really liked best? You probably didn't notice him. A short, fat man carrying a pork pie with a flag in it, saying 'Peace for all Pigs!' It turned out he was from the Society of Vegetarians.
Lois laughs.
GIDEON: Oh, that's marvellous! Yes, that's really the best!
LOIS: They were all fasting, you know. Everyone in that square, I bet you.
DAVID: That girl in the string mini looked like she'd been fasting for a month.
LOIS: What's that smell?
Pause. They sniff.
DAVID: Cooking.
LOIS: It can't be.
GIDEON: Oh, I think it can. [*Slight pause. He calls*] Mark!
Mark enters from the kitchen, wearing an apron, a chef's hat made out of newspaper, and carrying a cooking-slice.
MARK: You called for me, sir?
GIDEON: Peace.
MARK: How are you? Rumour reached me that people threw things at you.
GIDEON: [*calmly*] Only a few. It's not the first time the

League of Empire loyalists has emptied its rubbish over the British public. Besides, I was in wonderful hands. These two looked after me all day, like the brave fliers they are!

LOIS: Nonsense, Giddy. He was just great, Mr Askelon! You should have seen him! His head was like the still centre of that whole huge crowd!

GIDEON: Well, it didn't feel very still, or very central, come to that!

MARK: Why? Did you fast badly?

GIDEON: Not at all. I saw two members of Parliament, who had obviously just left the dining room of the House of Commons. I thought they looked at me with envy.

LOIS: You should have a good hot bath and go straight to bed. I'll run it for you.

GIDEON: [staring at Mark] In a moment. You appear to be cooking something.

MARK: Yes. I'm a weak brother, I regret to say. I held out all day, out of sympathy. But just fifteen minutes ago, I yielded. I'm afraid I started to make myself the very smallest repast. Of course, I'll eat it out of sight, in there.

He makes to go back to the kitchen.

GIDEON: Mark.

MARK: Yes?

GIDEON: Bring your very small repast in here. Please.

MARK: [grinning] Certainly.

He goes out. They all watch the kitchen. David squats on the floor. Mark re-appears, without his hat and apron, and carrying a laden tray.

Here we are.

He seats himself at the table, shakes out a white napkin, and tucks it under his chin.

A couple of lamb chops. What could be more sustaining?

LOIS: [shocked] Lamb?

MARK: Bought in the village, this afternoon! [He uncovers them] Behold them – beautifully crisped in the English manner. With them, one salad of watercress prepared in the French. One hot roll, leaking butter into a sympathetic napkin. One bottle of Corton, 1964. Your bin is woefully spartan, Giddy. I took the liberty of replenishing it by tele-phone. [*He raises the Greek cup*] Well, here's to famine! Self-willed famine, of course.

> *He drinks. David laughs. Lois throws him a look of outrage.*

[*To Gideon*] So. Were you impressive? Did you change hearts and collect minds?

> *Gideon comes and sits next to him.*

GIDEON: I hope so. In one way or another.

LOIS: He was cheered all day.

MARK: Were you?

GIDEON: Well, it was more people cheering up themselves, really. It keeps out the damp.

LOIS: [*smiling*] That's not true. When he got up to go, it was just deafening. Tomorrow they say there's going to be an even bigger crowd.

MARK: Are you going tomorrow, David?

LOIS: Of course he is! Why don't you change your mind and come too?

MARK: Were you fasting, David?

DAVID: I don't know. I didn't get anything to eat, anyway.

LOIS: What do you mean? Of course you were fasting. You agreed to it.

DAVID: I didn't say anything, actually. You told me I was.

MARK: [*blandly*] Well, would you like something now? There's this other chop here.

LOIS: [*indignantly*] He certainly would not! . . . [*To Gideon*] I saw this man from the *Observer* taking pictures like crazy. He was trying to get you to turn your head for half an hour. He'll be there again tomorrow.

GIDEON: Perhaps I should faint for him.

LOIS: Into my arms!

GIDEON: Excellent idea. It should make a brilliant poster. A Pietà, with the ages reversed!

> *David rises.*

DAVID: [*to Mark*] Thanks. I'll have it. [*Pause*] The chop.

> *He goes to the table.*

MARK: By all means. Here –

He forks one of the chops to Gideon, who sniffs it, interestedly, and passes it to David.

GIDEON: [*Imperturbably*]: Bon appetit.

DAVID: Thank you.

He sits. Lois glares at him.

MARK: Have some wine.

DAVID: No, thanks. Actually, I don't like alcohol much.

LOIS: He prefers pot.

MARK: You do?

DAVID: Yes. I think it's better for you. Or anyway, it does you less harm.

MARK: I've heard that argument before, my dear boy. It's merely pot calling the bottle black.

David laughs.

LOIS: I'll run your bath, Giddy. Please come upstairs.

She moves to the stairs.

GIDEON: Very well. [*To David*] You find that repulsive, don't you?

DAVID: [*his mouth full*] Yes.

LOIS: I hope it chokes you.

She goes upstairs.

MARK: Pacifism makes people so generous.

DAVID: She's alright.

GIDEON: She takes things very seriously, our Falcon.

MARK: Wisely.

He smiles at Gideon.

GIDEON: Excuse me.

He goes upstairs.

MARK: Well. Alone at last.

DAVID: Yes.

MARK: Am I . . . as you remember me?

DAVID: You've lost weight a bit.

MARK: With whom? [*He laughs*] It's well known, no one reads me any more. Mind you, there hasn't been that much to read recently. Unlike the productions from Shrivings. It's a veritable philosophy factory here! [*Raising the cup*] To home!

He drinks and hands it to his son, who also drinks.

DAVID: Home.

MARK: You're happy here, aren't you?

DAVID: Yes.

MARK: That's good. All the same, of course, you can hardly intend to remain forever. I mean, sooner or later, Shrivings is going to be full of furniture. Unless you are intending to start a workshop, and supply the area.

DAVID: [*smiling*] I'm not going to be a carpenter all my life, you know.

MARK: I hadn't actually imagined you were. What do you really want to be?

DAVID: I don't know.

MARK: You must have some ideas.

DAVID: They keep changing.

MARK: Well, let's hear some of them.

DAVID: Last week I wanted to be an old woman.

MARK: Yes?

DAVID: Living near here. Its strange, but the Cotswolds mean more to me than the Mediterranean. I suppose green turns me on, and yellow doesn't . . . I'd gone for a walk the other side of Trister. And there was this brick house with a sign saying Jam for Sale. The door was open and the wireless was playing. I could see it through the window. It was a real wireless – one of those Gothic ones, with fretwork on the front. I rang the bell and this woman came. She had red knuckles and hair-grips – you know, the old-fashioned, wavy ones. She saw me and smiled. Just like that. A huge smile, all National Health teeth: the way you can only smile, I bet you, if you've been there four hundred years. She was absolutely *there*. She wore great carpet-slippers, cut out at the toe for her corns, and they were part of the corridor, like the flagging. She weighed everything very solid in her hand, the jar of jam, the money I gave her, the latch on the door, and, you know something – the only word she said the whole time was 'Thank you'. Over and over. 'Thank you'. It was like a little flat song. 'Thank you for shillings. Thank you for cold. Thank you for greengages and hair-grips and the wireless. Thank you for asking the way'. . . . And suddenly I wanted to be her, more than anything else.

MARK: Good. I deserved it.

DAVID: What?

MARK: Mind your own business, father. You've forfeited the right to enquire.

DAVID: I didn't mean that!

MARK: I had no idea I had such a witty son. A charming way of telling me.

DAVID: That's not true!

MARK: Sssh! Not another word. I understand . . . Doubtless you find it easier to converse with Gideon. Well, naturally. Over a few months a giant intellect can learn anything, even the parlance of the young.

DAVID: You must know what I'm talking about. You *must*!

MARK: Well, I can learn. You'll have to teach me, of course. It's a new language – it always is – *young* English!

DAVID: *Don't*!

MARK: What?

DAVID: You said 'Home!'

MARK: [*hard*] And you've found it. Good!
    Silence. David looks away. Lois comes downstairs and crosses to the study with Gideon's clothes.

MARK: Ah, Miss Neal. The sage is laving himself?

LOIS: Sir Gideon is having his bath, Mr Askelon.

MARK: Washing the fascist tomatoes out of his hair!

LOIS: [*coming out of the study*] I'm afraid I don't find that very funny, sir. The man is quite exhausted.

MARK: It's entirely his own fault. He is hardly of an age to sit about on wet pavements.

LOIS: There are some things more important than physical comfort, sir.

MARK: What things in particular? What exactly has been achieved by today's nonsense? One old man lying dizzy in the bath-tub, instead of sitting down here eating a nice Welsh rarebit.

LOIS: That's plain silly! Excuse me, but it is.

MARK: Then what did he really do today? Tell me that.

LOIS: He made a sign.

MARK: And that's sufficient?

164

LOIS: When the first monk set himself on fire in Saigon, everyone in the so-called civilised world was suddenly aware of Vietnam. That was a sign. OK? Well, in a small way that man, walking out of that square tonight, being touched by hundreds of people – that was a sign too.
MARK: I declare you believe in the People, Miss Neal. How moving. It has a sublime simplicity – like Doric pillars, of bread and jam!
LOIS: Huh?
MARK: The poor tormented People, who left to themselves would make such a loving world! Exquisite.
LOIS: [*with an attempt at calm*] It is very easy, Mr Askelon, to put a person down by calling her simple. OK I'm simple. I'm naive, simple-minded American. I believe in the people, yes. And I believe that most of them don't want any part of the world they've been given. They don't want war. Or politics. Or organised religion. They've been taught to want these things by the ruling class, just desperate to keep its power. If they could ever get their heads straight, ordinary people would realise what history is all about. How it's just the story of a great big lie factory, where we're all been made to work every day, printing up labels: Serf. Heretic. Catholic. Communist. Middle-class. And when we're through, we're made to paste them over each other till the original person disappears, and nobody knows who the hell he is any more!
DAVID: [*admiringly*] Yes!
LOIS: Till we can't ever tear them off us again and just be the great thing you despise, Mr Askelon. People.
DAVID: Oh, when she talks like this I can listen all night.
MARK: I agree. It's better than the opera!
DAVID: [*Yorkshire accent*] Will ya marry me, Lois, lass?
LOIS: [*upset*] Oh, cut it out, David!
MARK: I'd take him up on it, if I were you. Not many girls get proposed to on the strength of their rhetoric.
LOIS: Ha, ha, ha! . . . Why did you come here, Mr Askelon? What do you want? . . . I used to admire you so much. I used to think you were one of the few real people in the world . . .

MARK: Used to!

LOIS: Boy, can you ever be wrong!

MARK: *Used to!*

LOIS: [*very near tears*] I must have been out of my mind!

MARK: *Used to admire! Used to!*

LOIS: I don't care what suffering you've had in your life! It doesn't excuse a damn thing!

MARK: Sagging Jesus – *Once!* The crucifixion of Once! You *said!* You *wrote!* You did *once!* . . . Nail a man to Once and cry when he drops, leaving his fingers on the wall! You arrogant little beast, do you imagine I live my life to be approved by *you?*

Lois turns away, dabbing furiously at her eyes.

DAVID: Stop it. Please!

MARK: [*hard*] What?

DAVID: [*embarrassed*] I mean . . . Well, that's not fair. Really.

LOIS: [*suddenly turning back on Mark*] Boy, oh boy, are you contemptible! The Grand Old Man, destroyed by suffering! When you're my age, you'll understand. Till then I can kick your head in all I like!

DAVID: Hey, hey!

LOIS: [*to David*] I tell you I don't know one person over fifty – except Giddy – who isn't full of shit!

Mark rises in apparent fury. She falls quiet. He approaches her.

Pause.

MARK: [*gently*] Who gave you those eyes?

LOIS: Huh? . . .

MARK: Blue as the jeans of innocence. Blue as fall sky above your Elysian Field, where the unicorn masses crop the grass of Universal love – till they're taken out by wicked keepers and shot . . . I'ts a lovely vision, Miss Neal. Many of us dreamed it once. And then woke.

LOIS: You didn't wake, Mr Askelon. You went to sleep for good.

Pause.

MARK: [*still very calm*] In 1920 the greatest psychiatrist in Europe analysed the dreams of five hundred patients. From

166

them, he slowly made out – detail by detail – the appalling shape of the Nazi beast. It was there, waiting to spring out of the black cave of the Common Unconscious . . . Out of that deep pit, stinking of orgasm, economical soup and the halitosis of mediocrity, have risen all the terrors of the earth. All the kings who now sit in museums, glaring at the tourists. The rulers of Assyria tearing lions in half. The despots of Asia, with their cold lozenge faces, forever denying forgiveness. The pop-eyed Lord of Sassania, primping his silver beard, saying 'Behold perfection! I have no petty thoughts. No haemorrhoids. No moments when I fail to get erection. Long live the King! The King *must* live forever!' . . . Who would make such objects? God cannot make anything infallible. Who needs Forever? Who raised these idols from the anonymous dust – hysterical puppets of Ninevah or Nuremberg? Who linked the wires? Started the sceptre arms flailing, the saluting arms of self-abuse? Who opened their anthem-yelling metal mouths? Who if not I? Him. You. [*Pause*] You walk royal portrait galleries as if you are attending identity parades for murderers. Start looking for yourself there, Miss Neal. You might just begin to understand history better.
  Lois stares at him, fascinated.
DAVID: Oh hey! Thank you! Wow!
LOIS: What do you mean?
DAVID: The words.
LOIS: What do you mean, 'wow'?
DAVID: The words . . .
LOIS: So it's wow for Giddy and wow for him and wow for me and wow for everybody with you?
DAVID: Yes!
LOIS: No distinctions! No differences at all?
DAVID: Well, you screw up your mouth too much. It doesn't do a thing for your face.
LOIS: What?
DAVID: You don't have enough moments that only happen once. You should have more.
LOIS: I think you're mad.
DAVID: I mean, to turn tummies over.

LOIS: I really do! Life's just a set of pictures to you, isn't it? What we say here doesn't connect with you at all.

DAVID: Pictures connect.

LOIS: You know what that means?

DAVID: Pictures are real.

LOIS: It means you have a complete inability to feel anything not related to personal gratification.

DAVID: Really?

LOIS: Yes, really. I'm sorry for you, David.

DAVID: Thank you.

LOIS: I really am. Anyone who can't feel social injustice is sick. I mean it!

DAVID: [*exploding*] Alright! You mean it! You really pity me! Poor me! Poor bloody me! [*He springs up and pulls a 'mad' face at her*].

LOIS: David. Ssh!

DAVID: Alright, I'm insane! [*He rushes to the table, stands on it, grabs some watercress out of the salad bowl, and puts it on his head. He flicks some watercress at her*]. Deficient Dan, the Insane Man!

LOIS: Stop it!

DAVID: Couldn't feel things, so away he ran!

LOIS: Stop it, David! Cut it out!

DAVID: [*quietly*] You stop it. Stop picking . . . Mad people shouldn't be picked on!

MARK: No, but heretics should. [*Standing up*] And that's what you are, my boy. A raving, flagrant heretic, ripe for the burning. Don't you realise what you have just admitted?

DAVID: [*shyly*] No.

Mark moves to David.

MARK: A sense of the Unalterable. Oh my poor, demented son: in this house that is enough to get you stoned to death and buried in the midden! [*Kindly*] Give me some watercress too! Let me go down with you under the knives of optimism! [*He plunges in his hand, takes out some watercress and jams it on his head too*] Acolytes of the unalterable: unite! Let's wear our green with courage! Green for Nature! For the returning cycles of our agony! The grazing green of God!

David laughs. Mark begins to walk about, enjoying himself, crowned with greens.

Ssh! You'll upset Torquemada . . . Isn't it amusing how the fashions in Inquisition stay the same! They all have one thing in common. A passion for invisible Gods. First we had vengeful Daddy, wrapped in clouds. Then Mobile Mary, whizzing up to Heaven. Now it's Self-Raising Man, jumping himself out of Nature: what an astonishing sight! . . .

Gideon appears on the stairs, dressed in a long white linen bathrobe. He halts, staring at the scene – then comes down into the room.

But perhaps I'm being unfair. No one ever saw Airborne Intacta on her jet flight to Jehovah – but with the God of Shrivings we may be luckier. Anytime now we might see something. Maybe today! Who knows? In a few hours the birds up there on Lyssop Ridge will be piping up a new morning. And the hands of perfectable Man will flutter out of sleep to begin again his wonderful work of self-creation. The hands of police will stir and pick up clubs. The hands of nuns will resume whipping fables into frightened children. The hands of patriots will tie some more electrodes onto partisan balls. The hands of the envious will load fresh guns, to assassinate hands more graceful than their own. And the delicate, nicotined hands of genius will continue to stuff all ages together – Dark, middle, and decayed – into one metal sausage. Hail to Man! Homo Improveabilis!

GIDEON: Smug!

MARK: What?

GIDEON: Smugness! The endless smugness of pessimism! Under all that litany of woe I heard only one note: *relish!* Comfort in the idea of your own perpetual failure. How can you receive that, and still have anything to live for?

MARK: [*grandly*] I do not require anything to live for!

GIDEON: Then you are unique in the world.

MARK: On the contrary, like everybody else, I live NOT to understand!

GIDEON: [*sharper*] Then why demand of me a Faith you *can?* You want an Indefinable God, but *I* must produce a definable

169

Man. Trot him out of a shed for your inspection, like one of your icons on a trolley! How unfair you are! . . . I offer you what you want. An indefinable mystery. This hand.
He extends it.
MARK: Offer me first one proof it can do better.
GIDEON: Its change of ownership.
MARK: What d'you mean?
GIDEON: Two thousand years ago, when it chained men all their lives to galley ships – one thousand, when it blinded an entire Byzantine army – five hundred, when it pushed men on to fires, and gutted whole towns to impose True Religion – it was the Gods' hand: plural or singular! Its crimes were accepted. They were God's will – God's scourge – God's anything, so long as they kept its owners from shame. Since we started to abolish Independent God, we have become measurably less callous.
MARK: [*sarcastic*] Oh, good!
GIDEON: It *is* good! Concern has its evolution. That's good.
MARK: Marvellous! We weep more – we war more. What a liberating equation! Agonize while you atomise!
GIDEON: We do not war more. It is only techniques that bring us to holocaust.
MARK: [*derisively*] Only!
GIDEON: [*bursting out*] Yes, only! *Only!* . . . I say again: concern has its evolution. Everything in *us* can have *unending* evolution. That is our glory – our amazement! . . . [*Scornfully*] How *can* you dish out that gloating old rubbish about the Unalterable? You ought to be ashamed! If we know *one thing* about Man, it is that he cannot *stop* altering – that's his condition! He is unique on earth in that he has *no* fixed behaviour patterns! Look at the world. At the differences in families – in tribes and nations. Some are paternal: some are not. Some are predatory: some are not. Some are aggressive, sustained by the desire to dominate others. Alright, but equally others are not. Oh yes, they can be *made* to be. These differences are social – but they are not inherent. They are not *biological.* Do you follow, children? . . . [*He turns to them*].

There is no proof whatever that man is born inherently aggressive.

MARK: [*ironically*] No proof?

GIDEON: [*sternly*] None. And I deny it, absolutely. Man is born free to make himself . . .

He approaches Mark, again extending his hand.

[*Urgently*] This hand – this is your proper focus for worship. Not glaring idols, or ancestor poles, or mothy banners hanging in cathedrals. This. This tool, for making. . . And soon to be extinct if we pursue our blasphemies against ourselves much longer.

He is moved, and stands staring at Mark as if challenging him not to agree. Mark takes Gideon's hand, and inspects it closely.

MARK: [*with disgusted interest*] In the Middle West of America, I watched this thing kill a man, seventeen times in succession.

GIDEON: You saw a man killed seventeen times?

MARK: [*dropping the hand*] Yes. What kind of evolution do you call that?

GIDEON: How?

MARK: In the psychology department of a major university, where they were working on aggression. The professor had set up a board with six buttons. These were allegedly controlled by electrical wires attached to an actor, sitting across the laboratory, bound and gagged. Members of the public, chosen off the street, completely at random, were admitted one by one and asked to assist at a scientific experiment of an undisclosed nature. They were told the first button would give the man a mild electric shock – the second more – and so on, up to the sixth, which was, in fact a death button. It was clearly explained to all that if they pressed that button the man would die. They were then left alone for an hour each, to play . . . A simple scene: one helpless man at the mercy of a complete stranger who was his absolute master in the matter of the punishment given him.

GIDEON: And seventeen pressed the death button?

MARK: Exactly so.

GIDEON: Out of how many?

MARK: Seventeen.

LOIS: I don't believe it.

GIDEON: [*patiently*] My dear, there is a famous experiment of this sort: but it wasn't exactly as you described. There was no death button. And the people were not left alone. They had two pseudo-colleagues – fake scientists whose job it was to provoke them. The result was that more than half agreed to vote for painful shock. Depressing, I admit, but scarcely as final as you make it out.

MARK: That was one experiment. I watched another.

GIDEON: [*dryly*] I see.

LOIS: I don't believe you. Go on, admit it. You made it up. You're reduced to making up stupid lies! How incredible.

MARK: Am I?

LOIS: Yes, you are!

GIDEON: Lois, please!

MARK: [*staring at her*] It's easily proved.

LOIS: Proved? How?

MARK: Sit down. We'll play my game here.

GIDEON: Here?

MARK: Why not? These apples will do very well.

> *He takes them from the bowl on the table, and lays them out in a straight line, parallel to the audience.*

The buttons of Original Sin! Ouch – oucher-oucher – Death! What do you say? Will you play ? I'll be the victim.

LOIS: You mean you'll act?

MARK: Exactly so.

LOIS: You've got to be kidding.

MARK: Try me and see. David?

DAVID: I'd like to see you act.

MARK: Good. Giddy? I can devise a short version for you, if you are tired.

GIDEON: I don't see how you can devise *any* version, my dear. We know you will be acting – and those are apples. The illusion that we can actually kill you being destroyed, there seems little point in the exercise.

MARK: Well, I would have to claim a few rights in compensation, denied to the original victim.

GIDEON: Of what nature?

MARK: Speech.

GIDEON: That seems fair.

MARK: Free speech. Complete license, no matter how provoking. Strictly of course for the purpose of the game.

GIDEON: That could be interesting.

LOIS: I don't see how.

MARK: Shall we try?

LOIS: I think it's time Giddy was in bed.

GIDEON: All the same, I would like to see what Mark intends.

MARK: Of course you would . . . Alright, then.

He pulls from his pocket the string with which he had wrapped the shrine.

Ah now, this will do very well! Come, David: tie me to your throne of reason.

He sits in it, and offers the string. David approaches.

Come on. Tie down the wrists.

David takes the string. He begins to tie.

LOIS: I don't see the point of this. I don't see the point of it at all. It's just plain stupid.

MARK: The head of the house wishes it. As I understand things, what he wants, so want the rest of you. Isn't that true?

LOIS: Ha, ha, ha!

GIDEON: Come on now, you fierce Falcon: it's only a game. An after-fast entertainment!

MARK: Exactly: only a game. Whatever that word means . . . Tighter, David: anyone can see I can get out of *that* . . . You do allow me complete licence of speech, by the way, Gideon?

GIDEON: Yes.

MARK: Miss Neal?!

LOIS: Why not? I guess there won't be any difference from the sort of things you say normally.

MARK: David?

DAVID: Anything you want . . . Can you move?

MARK: [*wriggling about*] No, that's fine. You might have made this chair especially for the purpose. To incapacitate your old dad! Alright, join the others.

David goes to the others, standing by the table.

You are, of course, all playing at once. The solo, masturbatory element has been eliminated. You must admit, I'm making it very difficult for myself.

GIDEON: I certainly admit that. Yes.

LOIS: What are you going to do? Just insult us till one of us bangs this last apple?

MARK: More or less.

LOIS: Jesus! I've never heard anything so stupid! Grown people standing up in the middle of the night, playing with apples.

GIDEON: Which is the mildest one?

MARK: The far one from me.
Gideon goes to it and raises his hand to touch it.

LOIS: [*with sudden alarm*] Giddy – don't.

GIDEON: Why not?

LOIS: Well . . . it's just so childish. [*Pause*] Goddam childish, that's all.

GIDEON: Let's oblige our guest. Don't you want to see how he acts?
Lois shrugs her acquiescence.

LOIS: OK. Go ahead.
Gideon delicately presses the first apple. Mark writhes a little.

MARK: Ah! Ah! Stop it, please.
Gideon stops pressing.

GIDEON: Excellent. Thank you.
The two men bow at each other.

LOIS: I don't think it's excellent! I think it's lousy. I've seen people under electric shock. It doesn't look at all like that.

MARK: Trust you to introduce a boring, factual note into the proceedings.

GIDEON: Really, Mark!

MARK: [*apologetically*] License, Giddy! License!

LOIS: What does the second button do?

MARK: Push it and see.

LOIS: I don't want to waste my money. What do you do? Twice as much?

MARK: Push it and see.

LOIS: Because that would only be twice nothing!

MARK: Push it and see.

LOIS: OK. Just this next one. Just to see how you make out. Look everybody – Acting Class Number Two! Bang! [*She bangs the second apple*].

Mark writhes more.

Presenting Mark Askelon, the greatest actor of our time, in – 'The Electrified Man!' . . .

Mark stops writhing.

Why are you stopping, Mr Askelon? I haven't taken my hand off the button!

Mark resumes writhing.

MARK: Ah! Ah! . . .

LOIS: There we go! Now you, Giddy! – you press number one again, and let's watch the subtle way he changes!

Gideon hesitates.

Go on, it's only a game. Like you said!

GIDEON: True.

LOIS: OK, then!

He presses the first apple again, and she takes her hand off the second. Mark's convulsions lessen.

Oh, beautiful! Beautiful! . . . Now mine again!

Gideon stops pressing and she resumes. Mark writhes more energetically, and his cries increase.

Now you, David! Press Number Three. He should really blow his mind on number three! [*To Mark*] Go on, keep it up! I'm still pressing! . . . Come on, David!

David hesitates.

What's the matter with you? We're just having fun!

David shrugs, smiles, shakes his head. Lois takes her hand off her apple. Mark relaxes.

You really are a pain in the ass, aren't you?

MARK: You certainly are, David. For once I agree with Miss Neal. I was enjoying myself hugely. And it is only a game, after all. That's why Miss Neal could afford to reveal herself so completely.

LOIS: What do you mean?

MARK: For one moment there, when you realised that I had

175

to keep writhing for just so long as you kept pressing, you became interested.

LOIS: Sure, I did. The longer I did it, the bigger fool you looked.

MARK: That's not the reason you did it, Miss Neal. Not by any means.

LOIS: Well, what other reason could there be, Mr Askelon?

DAVID: [*distressed*] Oh, stop it, Lois!

LOIS: What?

DAVID: Stop it.

LOIS: Thanks! Thanks very much. That's great. That really is great! . . . You tell me I'm so serious, and I'm too serious, and when I play a game you say Stop it.

DAVID: You weren't playing a game.

LOIS: Well, what the hell else was I doing? . . . I'm bored with this, Giddy. Why don't we go to bed?

MARK: Ah, that's sweet. 'Why don't we go to bed?' Can you really mean that seriously – to a man you've selected entirely because he can't?

GIDEON: Mark, really!

MARK: Well, it's true, isn't it? Look at her – Miss Lois Neal! What the hell is she doing in this house? Making the beds, making the eggs, making the laws round here like a sort of Earth Mother – or sorry: Earth Auntie. Unmarried, of course.

GIDEON: Mark, I must protest.

MARK: License, Giddy – license!

GIDEON: All the same! –

MARK: Who is she, this Illinois idiot, creaming her committed little panties every time you enter the room? [*American accent*] 'Oh, Giddy you're so great! Gee, Giddy, you're so wonderful! You're a fuckin' saint, boy, honest!' . . . Is that what you really want? A sticky little acolyte plunging after a man three times her age, just because he's safe?

All the others stay rigid: David, head lowered, Lois looking away.

What's in your mind, Lois? His wife couldn't stand it, could she? Stuck it three years after his famous vow of chastity –

then ups and bloody goes. But you're made of sterner stuff than that, aren't you? You're going to last forever! Forever deliciously unsatisfied! Forever a Vestal Vigin, waving the flag of Humanity high over your frozen Mount of Venus! Sagging Jesus, protect me from all Liberal American Virgins!

GIDEON: David, please untie your father. I find I am tireder than I thought.

MARK: You granted me license.

GIDEON: Yes, and now withdraw it. Goodnight.

MARK: [*sotto voce, to David, who is approaching the chair*] Keep still.

GIDEON: Come, Lois.

MARK: Yes, come, Lois – before you hear any more. Before you hear, for example, why exactly Enid left! . . . Do you imagine it was because of that boring vow of chastity? You must, as they say, be joking! Enid Petrie never cared about sex. To her it was always 'nasties'! She's much happier now with her middle-aged accountant. One dry kiss at night before they skin the Ovaltine! She didn't leave Shrivings for *that*! . . It was the hypocrisy she couldn't take. Poor old stick, in her own way she had a sort of maidenly integrity.

GIDEON: [*facing him directly*] What are you talking about?

MARK: Do you have to ask? . . . Why do you imagine, Miss Neal, that your employer gave up sex? Because he found you ladies such a block on his path to virtue? Don't you know the only sex Gideon ever really enjoyed was with boys? Slim brown boys with sloping shoulders. He used to chase them all over Italy on our walking tours. And then, of course, the guilt would chase him: and I'd have to endure boring vows of repentance all the next day – to be broken again, naturally, all the next night, in the very next piazza! In the end he gave everything up. Guilt, nothing but guilt! The world saw only a Great Renunciation on the grandest philosophic grounds: but not so Enid. All she saw was a self-accusing pederast, pretending to be Ghandi!

DAVID: [*low*] Stop it.

MARK: Mind you, old habits die hard. Once you grow accustomed to having Mediterranean boys, I suppose you get to

177

need them. Send for them. Import them. Steal them, if necessary, from your friends!

DAVID: [*in pain*] Shut up.

MARK: Make my chairs! Make my tables! Make my bed, and we will lie on it together!

DAVID: [*moving forward*] Shut up!

MARK: Not, my dear boy – my flier! my *owl*! – that I would suspect *you* of anything so bizarre! Innocent to the last breath, I make no doubt!

David rushes to the table, picks up the 'death apple', and smashes it down over and over again. Pieces fly about the room.

DAVID: SHUT UP! SHUT UP! SHUT UP! SHUT UP!

MARK: [*triumphantly*] What?! Oh! – AAAHHH!!!

He 'dies' in elaborate convulsions. All freeze. Pause.

Then, with a violent motion, Mark snaps the ropes from his wrists and rises from the throne. With a grin at Gideon, he flaps like a great eagle up the stairs into his room. Pause again. Then David drops the bit of apple still in his hand and walks very stiffly out of the house. The front door slams. Lois turns round at this. Gideon approaches her, his arms outstretched – but with a stifled cry, she avoids them, and runs into the garden. Gideon is left standing alone. He bows his head over the table. The lights go down a little below, and come up above, where Mark is kneeling to the shrine.

MARK: I begged him! You heard. I *begged* him, over and over. 'Let me go. No questions'. He wouldn't believe me. Like you. You never saw me, either. I was literally invisible to you. [*Piteously*] The two of you. *You can't see!* [*Pause*] And then when it happens, you look at me with that stare of unbeliev-able pain. *He* will, too. Soon now.

He stands up. Gideon moves towards his study. He is upset and alarmed. He pauses at the throne, fingering the ropes that still hang from it. Mark pours himself a glass of brandy.

Thing is, I didn't believe me either, last night. I only half meant it, the battle. My usual half-meant, *you know* . . . And now it's here. The knife's in. Suddenly there's blood dripping in the house. Surprised blood . . . No return . . .

Gideon moves slowly to his study door, opens it – looks back at the room, and disappears.

[*darkly, to the shrine*] I begged you, too. 'Proteggimi' – remember? Look after me. What does that mean? Look after? What language do you speak, then, Saint? . . . [*bitterly*] Saint . . . Saint . . . SAINTS!

He throws the brandy in the face of the statue. It drips from the shrine as Mark turns away from it, and stands with head sharply averted.

SLOW BLACKOUT

2. Sunday Morning

Ten o'clock. The telephone rings insistently. Lois is tidying the room – picking pieces of apple off the floor. She ignores the telephone. Finally it stops. Her whole manner is shocked and cold.

Gideon comes in from his study and looks at her. He appears tired, and is dressed very casually: as if he has become involved with his clothes by accident.

Above, Mark lies inert on his bed.

GIDEON: Peace.

LOIS: Sure.

GIDEON: Who was that on the phone?

LOIS: I don't know.

GIDEON: Oh. How are you feeling?

LOIS: Fine. You?

GIDEON: It hasn't been a very pleasant night for any of us, I imagine. Where's David?

LOIS: I don't know.

Pause.

I want you to do something for me.

GIDEON: Certainly. What?

LOIS: [*hard*] Tell that man to go.

GIDEON: I can't do that, my dear.

LOIS: You have to.

GIDEON: There is no have to. We can't throw people out of here. Least of all him. If this house can't overcome what's happened to Mark, then it's useless.

Pause. She dusts.

Look: he asked us all yesterday what would happen if a ruffian came in here with a pistol. We all said we wouldn't fire back, didn't we?

LOIS: [*short*] Yeah.

GIDEON: Well, it's as simple as that. As complex as that.

LOIS: Yeah.

GIDEON: What can we do, but try and disarm him another way? Aggression is like a fire: smother it in blankets, it dies for want of air. Our blanket is acceptance.

LOIS: Yeah. O.K.

GIDEON: I know it sounds hopelessly abstract, after last night – but what else are we here for? You left America for one reason; the Peace men were joining in the violence. Well, is that what you want me to do now?

She goes on dusting.

Or is it something else? What he said about me.

LOIS: [*flat*] Don't be ridiculous.

GIDEON: No, be honest now.

David comes downstairs.

DAVID: Hallo. How are you feeling?

GIDEON: Peckish.

DAVID: Me too. [*to Lois*] Good morning.

No reply.

Peace.

LOIS: [*to Gideon*] I've got some letters to do. Excuse me, please. The car will collect you at twelve, same as yesterday. The assembly point will again be the statue of Charles the Third.

GIDEON: First.

LOIS: Big deal.

GIDEON: [*sympathetically*] Lois!

DAVID: What the hell's the matter with you?

LOIS: If you don't know, I'm not telling.

DAVID: Well, I don't know.

She pauses a second, then marches across and picks up a piece of apple.

LOIS: This, then. This, David.

DAVID: The apple?

LOIS: You really think that was a smart, civilised thing you did last night?

DAVID: Well, it stopped the voice.

LOIS: Voice?

DAVID: That was supposed to be the point.

LOIS: The point, David, was not to touch the goddam thing. You deliberately played his game.

DAVID: It shut him up, didn't it?

LOIS: Ha, ha, ha!

DAVID: Well, didn't it?

LOIS: OK. It shut him up! Well done! Great.

DAVID: So what's the matter? It was just an apple.

LOIS: 'Just' an apple!

DAVID: Yes! An apple is an apple is an apple.

LOIS: And an idiot is an idiot!

GIDEON: [*mildly*] Children, please. I beg you.

DAVID: I'm sorry, Giddy.

LOIS: I'll go answer letters. [*She moves to the study*].

GIDEON: [*calmly*] Before you go, I would like to make a brief observation about homosexuality. I mean, my own.

Slight pause.

DAVID: I think that's a boring subject.

GIDEON: Nevertheless, since it's been raised.

LOIS: OK. What about it?

Pause.

GIDEON: How to put it? . . . When I was young, I had, as they say, sex on the brain. I meant by that, that even when I worked on equations, or read Political Science, the impulse of my attention was somehow sexual. Sex was everywhere. A girl's hair bobbing down the street. The sudden fur of a boy's neck. The twitching lope of a red setter dog. In flowers, even – the smell of cow parsley in a field of poppies would almost make me faint. To say I was bi-sexual would have been a ludicrous understatement. I was tri-sexual. Quadri. Quinti. Sexi-sexual, you might say!

David laughs and sits on the floor, to enjoy it.

I tell you this, just in case you've been wondering about the guilt attributed to me last night. So far was I from feeling that particular emotion, I confess throughout my twenties I cheerfully, and indeed gratefully, engaged in repeated encounters with both sexes.

DAVID: [*gleefully*] Which did you prefer?

GIDEON: Boys were physically more attractive to me: their

lines are more economical. But for sex I preferred girls. In that department, at least, God got his mathematics right!

David laughs again. Lois does not laugh.

However – after fifteen years' abstinence, I find the whole area of experience somewhat remote. That is why, my Owl, though you are extremely attractive, I hope you won't find it unforgivable in me not to have responded more vigorously to your charms. You too, of course, my Falcon.

David springs up happily.

DAVID: I'm not sure. I think we should both be very offended! [*Warmly*] Oh, that's lovely! . . . You're lovely. You are! [*He hugs the old man*].

LOIS: All the same, you stopped.

GIDEON: True.

LOIS: It couldn't have been that great, if you stopped.

GIDEON: I describe intensity, not joy. You might not conceive it of me, but in those days I knew great violence. It grew, I think, from what used to be called Despair. The great Myth of sex told of coitus and transfiguration. Co-mingling of spirits! I found the reality to be very different. This supreme experience of union appeared to me with more and more force each time, to be simply a twin act of masturbation, accompanied by murmurs designed to disguise the fact. Out of that realisation, slowly, came a sort of cruelty. Having and discarding. Searching ever more mechanically, in a savourless frenzy of disappointment. I grew to hate the very shape of desire. Its parody of closeness. Its separating climax. Finally, I came to know that for me, it was the main source of aggression. That before I could even start on my innocence, I would have to give it up . . . My wife left me for the reason I have always told you. The decision was too rigorous for her. I didn't blame her. How could I? I myself found it . . . very difficult . . . Almost unendurable, in fact.

Pause.

The youngsters who come here find this all absurd, no doubt. Sex is no problem to them. Or so they tell us, anyway, with their tulip heads like emblems for tenderness. Can it be true? I pray so. If they can really kiss without the taste of conquest, then they've done more than all generations before them: detached the whip at their belts, and hung a flower ... So ... Everyone has a struggle. That was something of mine.

DAVID: Thank you.

Pause.

DAVID: [*enthusiastically*] Let's go for a walk. All three of us!

Mark stirs on his bed.

GIDEON: [*to Lois*] Yes! We have the time, my dear.

LOIS: You two go. There's too much I've got to do here.

DAVID: Well, leave it.

LOIS: I'm afraid I can't do that.

DAVID: Oh, balls!

LOIS: Shrivings does not run itself, David. Excuse me. [*She goes into the study*].

GIDEON: What's wrong?

DAVID: She's shocked.

GIDEON: Impossible. By what? My language? But she's such a free girl. She couldn't be shocked just by words. Not a liberal girl like my Falcon! Do you really think she found me coarse?

DAVID: I love you. I wish I could keep you from harm.

GIDEON: Am I in danger?

DAVID: Don't you feel it?

GIDEON: I feel ... a little unnerved. Perhaps it's the fast.

Mark gets off his bed and comes to the window. He stares out front.

DAVID: You didn't sleep last night.

GIDEON: No.

DAVID: You're changing.

GIDEON: What d'you mean?

DAVID: So's Lois.

Pause.

DAVID: That's the thing.

GIDEON: What?

David shudders.

David!

DAVID: He changes you. But he can't change himself.

GIDEON: I don't think that's true. He's changed more than

any of us. I never realised he had become so desperate.

DAVID: Become?

GIDEON: Well, yes, in the last few years. Was that what you were trying to tell me, before he arrived? You suspected this had happened?

DAVID: Not become.

GIDEON: What d'you mean? He was always like this? . . . That's nonsense, my dear. He was often trying – bombastic – egocentric – all of that. But never . . . never like this.

David shrugs.

What did you mean before? You wanted to stop the voice?

DAVID: The thing in it.

GIDEON: What thing?

David shrugs again.

I'm not sure I understand you.

DAVID: [*fiercely*] *The thing!*

Pause.

GIDEON: [*perplexed*] He would never hurt you. You know that.

DAVID: Let's go for our walk.

He goes abruptly over to the garden exit, where the coats hang, and takes Gideon's scarf and beret.

GIDEON: David . . .

DAVID: [*handing him the beret*] Here.

GIDEON: Thank you. [*He puts it on*] If I asked him to leave Shrivings, would you like that?

DAVID: You can't.

GIDEON: You mean, I mustn't.

DAVID: I mean, you can't.

Gideon stares at him. David takes his hand.

[*Quietly*] Come on.

They go out together. Above, Mark stares out front.

MARK: Well, there they go. Father and son – hand in hand up the meadow. Touching! The whole hippy dream in one frame: old and young, leaping the generation gap like mountain goats! . . . Look, he's dancing. Our boy!

He turns away.

[*Bitterly*] Dances with Giddy, and I stay here with you. No, with myself. Alone. You'd be up there with them leading the

dance. 'Venga, vengate! Dance with me, San Marco!'
[*Pompously*] 'No, no, my dear Giulia, good heavens: – *dance*,
with my girth? You must be mad! . . . *You* dance: I'll watch.'
You laugh: I'll watch. You live: I'll watch and turn it all into
Literature. Literature counts, after all! It's so much more
important than life . . .

> *The telephone rings. Lois comes in from the study and*
> *answers it.*

LOIS: Look, mister: a Vigil *is* a public statement. What more
do you want?

> *She hangs up and goes listlessly to the refectory table.*

MARK: So who's left downstairs? The Innocent Abroad,
savaging her typewriter! Bashing out manifestos of love, with
hating little touch-type fingers!

> *Lois sits at the table, staring miserably ahead.*

I must say I'd like to give her some touch-typing myself.
One hour could change her life. What's she ever known,
after all, but student fumbling?

> *He sits on the bed.*

Why not? Superb move! Life in Shrivings would hardly be
the same ever after, that's for sure. How would the old man
take it? How would David? –

> *He breaks the thought, snapping at the shrine.*

Ah, don't be idiotic! I couldn't do it, anyway. Look at her!
The odds are a thousand to one. Richard the Third had
better with that dreary Lady Anne! . . . [*Slyly*] All the same.
There she sits – tighter than a Labrador limpet. Here I sit,
the well-known blade, not entirely rusted yet. One could
always see. The most anyone can say in the end, to God or
Man, is Let us see!

> *He gets up. He smiles.*

My move, I think.

> *He leaves the room and tiptoes down. At the bottom of*
> *the stairs he pauses, contemplating the girl.*

All alone, with your Remingtone?

> *She ignores him. He advances into the room.*

Are you still angry with me for last night? You shouldn't be.
Truth hurts – but in a house of Shriving, one should tell

nothing else. And then one should forgive. Isn't that the point of this house?

LOIS: Why don't you just get out of here?

MARK: Where? Back to Corfu?

LOIS: So long as it's away from me, I don't give a damn.

MARK: Now that, I'm afraid, is *untrue*. I think you lie in bed at night thinking a great deal about me.

LOIS: You're right. I do think a lot about you. Not necessarily in bed. Would you like to hear what I think about you, Mr Askelon?

MARK: Not at all. Mediocre descriptive powers are not necessarily improved by having a great subject to work on.

LOIS: You think you're the last representative of the Grand Manner, don't you? – all cooking and quotations! You wear your learning lightly. You got style. Well, let me tell you – most of the kids I know have more style in their assholes than you have in your whole drunken body.

MARK: And Gideon? Do they have more style than Gideon?

LOIS: Damn you, Mr Askelon! We were happy before you came.

MARK: Liar! I saw you the day I arrived, Anxious Annie clutching her nervous little fistful of attitudes. Happy? You haven't even been goosed by happy!

LOIS: Screw you!

MARK: What was my real crime? Showing your saint in a real light?

LOIS: Get out of here   that's all I want.

MARK: Look, stop hiding from it. Giddy is completely queer, for what that's worth. He never slept with a woman in his life.

LOIS: That's not true.

MARK: It's not in the least important. Who cares, after all?

LOIS: It's not true!

MARK: It's just a question of the facts. Boring, unilluminating facts.

LOIS: *It's not true!*

MARK: You have proof to the contrary?

LOIS: Yes.

   Pause.

187

MARK: How beautiful. What a delicious discovery! Women can be as gallant as men. *More* gallant in this instance. I didn't exactly think Giddy displayed much last night. The way he came to your protection.
LOIS: You're not worthy to wipe his ass.
MARK: Or rather – didn't.
LOIS: [*tight*] I don't need any protection.
MARK: 'I find I'm tireder than I thought.'
LOIS: What?
MARK: That was the most he could manage to say. 'I find I'm tireder than I thought.' Hardly the last word in gallantry.
LOIS: You couldn't begin to understand him. You couldn't begin!
MARK: [*admiringly*] You really are remarkable.
LOIS: What d'you mean?
MARK: After a scene like that – to defend him like that. Eyes sparkling. Breasts heaving . . . You're a Valkyrie.
LOIS: Get fucked.
MARK: Alright, I'm joking, a little. But it's true, when you say you don't need protection. You have an integrity that is absolutely scary. You know, you are the first person I've met – since I first met myself – who can really treat abstractions like lovers.
LOIS: [*drily*] Great.
MARK: I mean kiss them. Beat them for infidelity.
LOIS: Ha, ha, ha.
MARK: It's what my wife never dug. She couldn't cope with the simplest general idea.
LOIS: Her son has the same problem.
MARK: She would have adored you. Honesty excited her above everything. Her eyes would have widened on you. They were quite miraculous, you know. Round the pupils flared a sun-ring. In all other ways she was quite ordinary. A spindly, red-haired dancer from the Rome Opera, not actually very good. When she retired to live with me on pasta and poems, she grew less shapely – but her eyes never lost their light. God knows where she got them. Her father was a grey civil servant with eyes like a carp. Her mother's, two clams on a

plate of spaghetti. I can only conclude, therefore, that Giulia's were miraculous. Like yours.

LOIS: Oh, sure.

MARK: Who gave you those eyes? Some baby-faced doctor from the plains of Illinois? Not on your mid-Western life! Eyes are the sequins of grace. The angel sews them, when she calls.

Long pause.

LOIS: [*calmly*] Giddy's eyes are disgusting.

MARK: What?

LOIS: That white stuff. It's really awful. Why doesn't he do something about it? And the way they're never really *on you*.

MARK: [*slyly*] As if they're . . . out of focus?

LOIS: You're really very clever, aren't you?

He grins.

MARK: I was.

LOIS: Yeah, sure.

MARK: You don't know how clever I was.

LOIS: 'Once,' you mean? Once?

MARK: [*staring at her*] Yes. Once. [*Pause*].

LOIS: [*softer*] Will you go now, please?

MARK: I was someone amazing!

LOIS: Just leave me alone . . .

MARK: I was the world!

LOIS: Please! Get out of here! . . .

MARK: I knew an Encyclopedic Sympathy: there was nobody outside of *me*! I was the arriving lecturer – and the doorman who admits him, cringing. I was the Fabergé Prince – the traveller in undies – the teagirl who stands for eight repetitive hours between two steaming urns. I went to parade grounds, brisk in khaki. Returned at night, tired dandruff in an aching bus. I was the arch of the morning – Cream of Corelli – the indigestion of a wasted day! I was a replete, complete Man . . . but for one thing. I was never quite alive. [*Pause*] Inside me, from my first day on earth, was a cancer. An incapacity for Immediate Life. When I was a boy, the crowd at football matches jumped to its feet, shouting. All I could see was a ball and legs. At student dances, I hopped in silence. They

all said: isn't it exciting, the music? I grinned, but heard nothing. The only music I ever heard was words, and the clear thought of Gideon Petrie. When I yoked them, I became your admired Poet. I slew Generals. I drowned Presidents in spit. The insane Popes! The Rabbis of Repression! Oh, they kept me going for years, good hates – *the scapegoats for myself*. The only thing was, they ran out. Even atheism itself ran out, the moment I felt one poem as an act of worship. The next second – when I realised how worship demands the Present – then hell began. I was no longer a Revolutionary Poet. I was a self-ordained priest without a faith.
　　Pause.
Do you know what I'm saying? I have never lived *Now*. And that 'Never' makes crueller murderers, even than Christ or Country. Look into my eyes. What do you see? The envy? The endless living through others? Jealousy squinting through the glare of commitment? . . . There is where Vietnam starts. Don't sit on pavements to ban armaments: sit, if you must, to ban these eyes. They would kill Gideon, if they could, for his goodness. They would kill David for his instinct. Yes, my own son – as they killed his mother: Giulia. Poor girl, you are looking at a murderer. But don't be afraid. You're quite safe. You have nothing I want, you see.
　　She kisses him gently on the mouth. He draws back, then kisses her passionately. She throws her arms round him.

CURTAIN

ACT THREE

1. Sunday Night

Eleven-thirty. Above, Lois lies in Mark's bed, naked, under a sheet. Behind her, stands Mark, also naked and wrapped in a large white towel. He holds a bottle.

MARK: Are you awake?

LOIS: Mmm.

MARK: Then listen, Miss America. Go home. Forget Europe. She's old, wicked, and useless – like me. Purge her. Get her right out of you, if you want to live. Believe me, everything bad started here. The pox. The subjugation of woolly heads. The social layer cake, which God's hand alone is allowed to crumble. Above all, the Police State. That's our main gift to the world. We've never been without it. The helmetted thugs of Prussia. Hohenstauffen – Hohenzollern. All those Bourbon nights. The shadows of agents everywhere – Fouché spies in the arcades – Metternich men – the soutanes of insane Priests slipping through the twilight – Rome, with her tinkling bells, summoning us to avoid ourselves. Giddy's quite right . . . [*Fiercer*] Never forgive them. The kneelers! The followers of carriage axels. The motorcade boys. The smart saluters. The slow lookers through documents. The postillions of the state in dark glasses, now not even bobbing on cream horses, – just on mobikes! Not even in plumes, – just in perspex, crackling with transistors. Disembodied, uninteresting as the astronauts, their heroes. Assembled men! . . . We taught you the tricks, and you've made them shoddier. Get us out of you entirely! The hell with Europe. Get us out of you! . . . I'm pissed.

He hands her the bottle.

LOIS: You're fantastic. Do you know you've been talking all day?

MARK: And you keep sleeping. Well, naturally. Speeches of such preternatural tedium.

LOIS: Don't be silly. Hold my hand.

He moves to the bed, and holds it.

MARK: Look at your eyes. It's a joke.

LOIS: What is?

MARK: Your mouth all day long shouts Equality! But your eyes keep singing Uniqueness! You won't hear *them* demanding Equal Eyes For All Women!

She giggles, and drinks from the bottle.

If I could once make them in a poem, I'd never open my mouth again. Consider that.

LOIS: Sssh!

David comes from his room, pauses a second on the landing, then runs down the stairs. Lois freezes.

The boy is naked, save for a white towel: he carries another. He goes straight to Gideon's study and knocks on the door.

GIDEON: [*inside*] Hallo?

MARK: [*kissing Lois's hand*] Firm, typewriter-bashing little hand. I think I'd quite like to be that Remington.

LOIS: Oh, stop it now.

Mark laughs. Gideon opens the door. He is wearing his white dressing-robe.

DAVID: You're still wet.

GIDEON: [*coming out into the room*] I am a bit.

DAVID: Sit down, I'll dry you.

GIDEON: No, it's alright.

DAVID: Sit!

Gideon sits. David starts to towel his head.

MARK: We'll have to go down in a minute.

LOIS: No.

MARK: We must.

LOIS: I don't want to.

MARK: You're just going to stay here?

LOIS: Yes.

She turns away from him and throws the sheet over her head.

GIDEON: It was noble of you to sit with me today.
DAVID: Don't be silly.
GIDEON: You got even wetter than I did. You looked like an otter.
DAVID: I enjoyed it.
GIDEON: Did you?
DAVID: I think because Lois wasn't there. I mean, yesterday she looked at me the whole time, like she was challenging me to find it boring.
GIDEON: Your opinion matters to her.
DAVID: Do you mean that?
GIDEON: Of course. Otherwise you wouldn't have such power to upset her.
DAVID: I really am naive, aren't I?
GIDEON: Yes, if you mean unconscious of your charm. Now, you will be more conscious, therefore less charming.
DAVID: Life's depressing, isn't it?
GIDEON: No denying it.
    Mark stands up.
MARK: Come on, now. It's time you got up.
LOIS: [*under the sheet*] No.
MARK: They've been back fifteen minutes. Gideon will be wanting his dinner. He must be starving.
LOIS: He can get it himself.
MARK: That's not a very nice thing to say.
LOIS: Oh, leave me alone!
DAVID: Where the hell can she be?
GIDEON: I don't understand it.
DAVID: We held the car for ages.
GIDEON: She must have been walking, and not realised the time.
DAVID: I don't believe it.
GIDEON: Why not? It's a natural explanation. She wasn't exactly pleased with either of us.
DAVID: Lois would never forget a vigil.
MARK: Lois.
GIDEON: Then what? You mean, she did it deliberately?
MARK: [*harder*] Lois.
GIDEON: But why? Why on earth would she? . . .

David towels harder.
Gently, my dear!
DAVID: What's going on, Giddy?
GIDEON: Going on?
DAVID: What is it? What has he said to you?
MARK: Here!
He jabs her. She sits up.
LOIS: Cut it out!
They glare at each other.
GIDEON: [*gently*] Trust me, my dear.
DAVID: What about? Trust you what about?
GIDEON: You know, they say there are seven meals between Man and Revolution. I've missed six already.
DAVID: Poor Giddy. I'm sorry . . . I'll get you something right now. Let's see what there is. [*He crosses to the kitchen*].
GIDEON: She didn't even leave us any food ready. I can't think why.
DAVID: Because she's a selfish cow.
GIDEON: Sssh!
MARK: Get out of bed.
LOIS: No.
DAVID: You're alright, aren't you?
GIDEON: I think so. How about you! You haven't eaten either.
DAVID: I'll be better after a snack. Excuse me.
He goes out.
Mark comes over to Lois.
MARK: [*hard*] Get up, Lois!
LOIS: What's the matter with you?
MARK: I need you downstairs.
LOIS: Need?
MARK: Exactly.
LOIS: What *is* this? What game are you playing?
MARK: My own. As always.
LOIS: But I figure in it, don't I? You want me downstairs very much. Why?
MARK: Press it and see.
LOIS: [*realising it*] You're going to tell, aren't you? You're

going to tell, right now! . . . You are, aren't you? Why? . . .
Why?
MARK: Stop questioning me, you silly bitch! Put on your
panties and get downstairs.
LOIS: You've *planned* it! . . . You've planned the whole thing!
MARK: Let's have no hysterics, please.
LOIS: Every bit of it . . .
MARK: Lois –
LOIS: Every bit!
MARK: [*quietly*] I'll open the door. You can scream again.
He moves to the door.
LOIS: I'm not leaving this room. I'm staying right here.
MARK: As you please.
He leaves the bedroom and comes downstairs.
Good evening.
GIDEON: Peace.
MARK: How was your vigil? A smash-hit, I should imagine.
You *are* clever, making that addition to the story. I mean the
fast. Add the possibility that the leading actor might pass out
at any minute, and you turn the inevitable anti-climax of a
second-night performance into pure thriller. Congratulations.
GIDEON: I again missed you among the audience.
MARK: And Lois. You must have missed her too.
GIDEON: I did. Where is she?
David comes in, carrying a can of soup.
DAVID: I've found some lentil soup. It's only a tin –
He stares at his father.
MARK: Would you lay a place for me also? After all, it's an
occasion – the breaking of the Great Man's fast. Perhaps we
should call it the First Supper!
DAVID: It'll be five minutes, Giddy.
He starts to go back to the kitchen.
GIDEON: Lay a place for your father, too, please.
DAVID: Alright.
MARK: And for Lois too, please. She will be hungry also. [*He
smiles*] It's not only vigils that make man hungry.
DAVID: What?
MARK: Lay for your father, and he will lay for you.

Pause.
DAVID: Where is she?
They stare at one another. Intuitively, David moves to the foot of the stairs.
[*Calling up*] Lois? . . . *Lois!*
The girl starts up in bed.
MARK: Perhaps she's asleep.
DAVID: Lois!
The girl gets quickly out of bed, wrapping the sheet about her. Standing there, she drinks elaborately from the bottle.
GIDEON: [*to David*] Gently, David, I beg you.
DAVID: Lois!!!
Carefully, she puts down the bottle, winds the sheet around her, and comes slowly downstairs: a white figure joining three others.
GIDEON: Peace.
LOIS: Good evening. [*To David*] Good evening. [*To Mark*] Good evening. [*To Gideon*] You got wet.
GIDEON: I'm afraid I did.
LOIS: Well, that's alright. It was that kind of a day. Everybody got wet! . . .
She starts to wander round the room.
Actually, it was an ordinary day. Absolutely ordinary. Some people got chicken in their gut, and some people got a bullet, and some other people – the lucky ones they *say*, got something else. And it's all explicable only in the eyes of God. [*To Mark*] Right? . . . [*To David*] What are you doing with that? Are you going to give that to Giddy? Is that all he gets after two whole days' starvation – is that all he gets in *his* gut? – a lousy plate of canned soup? Ah, poor Giddy! I stop looking after you for one day, and see what happens. You see – you still need me!
She gives a strained laugh.
Well actually no one needs anyone. That's just a word – *needs*, one of those crazy words . . . mess up your head . . .
DAVID: Lois . . .
LOIS: [*fiercely snatching the can of soup out of his hand*] Give me that!

She turns and goes with it into the kitchen.
GIDEON: [*to Mark: cold*] What have you done?
MARK: [*innocently*] I?
GIDEON: I can't believe . . .
MARK: What?
GIDEON: Even . . . Even within the context . . . *No, Mark.*
MARK: What? What, Gideon?
GIDEON: [*bursting out*] That even you! –
MARK: 'Would stoop so low?'
He laughs. David turns and stares at him.
MARK: [*to his son*] What are you gaping at? An old wreck still attractive to women? Disgusting, isn't it? Pleasure's for the young. Everyone knows that! . . . Portrait of a teenager discovering the world not made entirely in his own image!
Pause. Mark sits on the throne.
Don't worry, boy! You didn't miss much. It wasn't exactly the sex act of the era. She's as cold as haddock, you must know that. Deep Freeze Dora, the Tundra Gash!
GIDEON: Be quiet!
MARK: Still, I gave her *something*. What do you think she wanted from you, eh? Drugs and shrugs, and a pleady kiss once a week. D'you think that satisfies a girl? I know you pot babies. It's all wow and wee-wee, with you, isn't it? You can't get it up to save your stoned lives!
GIDEON: Be quiet! Be quiet, this instant!
MARK: [*ignoring him*] No wonder she couldn't stand you – your mother. Even in her, deep down, was the natural Italian horror of the Unmale.
GIDEON: Mark, I beg you!
Mark gets up again. He approaches his son, and puts his arm intimately around his neck.
MARK: Now don't fret, boy. We're two of a kind, you and I. I could never dominate a woman either. You don't want to believe all that stuff about me, the Great Lover. It was all rubbish. I failed just as early with Giulia. Well, of course. All she wanted was the ancestral Roman pattern. Smashed fist: smashed plate. How else do you know you are loved? I was

hopeless at it! – her 'big shy Englishman'! It was my fault, really, she had to turn elsewhere for comfort.

David turns to him sharply. Gideon rises, appalled.

Oh well, yes! What's so new about that? What's the big surprise? You must have realised! No? . . . You mustn't be too hard on her. After all, what else was she going to do? She was a hot lady, your mum. What I couldn't supply, she had to get somewhere. So she found it in Corfu harbour. A vulgar choice, but there you are.

GIDEON: [*in pain*] Mark!

MARK: [*roughly*] Oh come on now, Giddy. Stop play-acting! It's time we told him.

GIDEON: 'We'?

MARK: My snot son, who claims no kinship with the Mediterranean! It's time he knew our little secret.

GIDEON: Secret? . . . What secret? . . . There's no – no – no secret! . . .

DAVID: [*soft: dead*] Stop it.

GIDEON: [*desperate and confused*] I know no secret, David!

David stands rigid, looking at neither of them.

DAVID: Just stop it, Giddy.

GIDEON: I know nothing, David. Believe me: nothing. He's inventing every scrap of this!

MARK: Oh, come now: you can do better than that! You don't have to resort to lies, Gideon. Protect him, if you want – but don't lie! It's shocking when *you* do it!

GIDEON: [*urgently*] David? . . .

MARK: It's really obscene!

GIDEON: Dear boy?

DAVID: [*low: stiffly*] Just stop it. Just stop the voice. The voice . . . The voice . . . *Please!* . . .

MARK: Look at you! Is that my face? Dirty olive out of the standard wop jar! Is that my body? Slack-waisted camel-walk: the harbour hump! Get with it, you lump of Italy – it took a lot of pasta to make you!

GIDEON: [*breaking out*] Be silent! Abominable – abominable man! Close your mouth!

MARK: You know it's true.

GIDEON: I know nothing of the sort. There's not one word of truth in any of this, and you know it. Believe me, David, not one!

MARK: Why, what's the tragedy? Some matelot lowered his flap to his mum under the arcade. So what? We're all God's bambini, aren't we?

GIDEON: Liar!

MARK: I forgave her. Gave you my name!

GIDEON: Liar!

MARK: My glorious *name* – which some girls still conjure with! . . . Alright, when you were young. But come thirteen, when she saw her little Corsican stoker or whatever he was, start to slouch round the villa, memory-sized – ah, then she got the Gods! Suddenly she couldn't bear to look at you any more! Started calling you her punishment. God's retribution on a Catholic girl who had strayed! You had to go, and I had to do it. Send you to England for your education. Keep you away from Corfu. Telegrams every few months – 'Still not convenient you return. Your loving father.'
David looks at him in horror.

GIDEON: Listen to me, David. All of this is part of a game. A hideous, disgusting game. Your father is simply trying to provoke me, that's all. That is all it's about.

DAVID: [*in anguish*] Just stop the voice, Giddy! Stop it, that's all I want!

MARK: [*raising his voice*] Why else should I keep you away from Corfu all those years? Answer me that! Why else should I keep you away for six whole years – if she hadn't begged me to? Why else would I do that, Giddy? Perhaps you can tell!?

GIDEON: I don't know. I don't care!

MARK: Why else?

GIDEON: Hold your tongue.

MARK: [*to David*] Why else? Why else? Give me one reason, my dear little bastard!

GIDEON: [*exploding*] No! . . . I order you! – I order you – YES! . . .

MARK: [*jeeringly*] What?
Pause.

GIDEON: [*controlling himself with great effort*] To be quiet.
Suddenly David runs to the garden exit, snatches up
his boots, and shoves his feet into them.
David! ... Where are you going?
DAVID: Away.
GIDEON: Where?
DAVID: Out of the voice.
GIDEON: No!
David runs towards the front door.
Stay here.
DAVID: I can't.
GIDEON: Please, David. *Please!*
DAVID: I can't, Giddy. No more!
GIDEON: All of this is lies. Every bit of it. Everything he says
is a lie!
DAVID: [*in great anguish*] I KNOW! I KNOW! *I KNOW!* ..
Slight pause.
GIDEON: [*with desperate quietness*] Then why?
DAVID: I've got to get out. That's all.
GIDEON: No. Not you! ... Not *you!*
MARK: Then who? Who's got to get out, then, Giddy? ...
Who?
A pause. Gideon wrings his hands.
GIDEON: No one. Everyone must stay. No one must leave
this house. No one.
He stands, looking straight ahead.
DAVID: [*dead*] That's right. No one. In the end, there's no
one. 'Be silent. Hold your tongue.' That's all you can do.
You can't stop it. The voice goes on and on – and all you've
got against it is words. Lovely words. And theories – lovely
theories. And fasts!
GIDEON: Owl!
DAVID: Theories and hopes and vigils and fasts! And
nothing! Lovely nothing!
GIDEON: David! ...
DAVID: [*savagely*] No one and Nothing!
He turns on his heel and moves to the stairs. Gideon
pursues him.

GIDEON: David! . . . Listen to me, I beg you. Please, David, – look at me, at least. My dear, dear boy – look at me. Please . . . Won't you look?
David turns.
DAVID: [*howling*] FUCK OFF!
He dashes upstairs. A pause. Gideon begins to move slowly downstage. Mark comes up to him.
MARK: Congratulations. The battle's over. You win. I see there is nothing I can do will make Shrivings reject me. You will even help torture a boy to maintain its foundations.
He opens his arms wide.
Master – Receive your Disciple!
Gideon stares at him, then crumples in a faint on to the floor. Mark crouches over him in horror.
MARK: [*in a whisper*] Giulia! . . .
He looks wildly about him, then retreats in panic to the stairs, calling aloud.
Lois! . . . LOIS!
LOIS: [*off*] What is it? [*She rushes in*] Giddy!
MARK: [*moving to the table*] Water . . .
LOIS: [*kneeling*] Giddy! . . . Jesus! . . . Giddy! . . .
She pulls him to a sitting position.
. . . Giddy!
MARK: [*approaching with the water*] Give him this.
LOIS: No!
MARK: It's only water.
LOIS: [*ferociously*] Get away! Don't you touch him! Get away!
Mark scrambles to the foot of the stairs where he watches her revive Gideon.
Hey . . . Hey now . . . Hey now, Giddy . . . Hey now . . . Open your eyes. Open your eyes for me, Giddy. Come on now: be good. Be good with me, Giddy . . . Be good . . .
She starts to rock him to and fro in her arms.
LOIS: Come on, now, be my Giddy: my own Giddy: my darling! Come on, now, be my Giddy: my own Giddy: my darling! Come on, now, be my Giddy: my own Giddy: my darling!
Gideon opens his eyes, and stirs.

Hi! You fell. It's alright. I'm here. Try and stand. Come on. Lean on me. Up we go . . . That's it . . .

She helps him to rise. Mark moves up the stairs into his bedroom, leaving the door open.

Now we'll sit over there. Come on. It's only a few steps . . . There we are . . . Come along now . . . That's it.

She leads him tenderly across the room to the table, and helps him sit behind it, facing front.

Now I'll make you some soup. It won't take a minute.

GIDEON: [*faintly*] No.

LOIS: Of course, my dear. You're very hungry. That's why you fell.

GIDEON: No.

LOIS: I'll bring you some bread, first. Just while I heat it.

GIDEON: Please leave me alone.

Mark suddenly raises his head and calls out:

MARK: David!

Gideon half rises.

LOIS: Giddy, please sit down. You haven't any strength at all. Go on, now.

He obeys her.

LOIS: You just sit there. I'll be right back.

She goes into the kitchen.

MARK: [*roaring*] David!

Gideon lowers his head and puts his hands over his ears. Suddenly David dashes out of his bedroom, crosses violently into Mark's room, and slams the door behind him. He glares.

[*Throwing out his arms*] Alright – I'm here. Look. Look. Look! Keep them on me, your eyes – your mother's – yes! Ruined by me! Who the hell else could I be but your dad? Keep looking. This is it. The last time. You'll hear the voice just once more – then never again. I'll go back to Corfu for life!

Father and son stare at each other, each dressed in white towels.

Now. Now – I'll tell you why I kept you out of your home.

He raises a bottle to his lips – then suddenly chucks it on the bed instead. David keeps looking at him.

Your first week on earth you stared at me like that. Before you could even see properly, you heard the voice. The dead man's voice, singing a lullaby. Your face wrinkled in fear.

Pause.

When you were six, I watched you race your bike through the olive trees. Your mother was standing beside me. Your mouth opened with glee. Hers too. All I got were the mouths opening and shutting. No glee. Just physical movements. I stood there hating you both. Filling up with hate. And you, twisting the handlebars, turned and caught my eye, you shook – and fell off. Giulia screamed and ran to you. I didn't . . . Do you still shake?

David stands unmoving. Mark turns away. Below, Lois comes in with a board of bread and a dish of butter.

LOIS: Here now. Have a slice of this.

Gideon does not move.

Don't give me a hard time now, Giddy. Sit up.

GIDEON: [*raising himself*] Please go away.

Determinedly, she cuts the bread and butters it.

LOIS: There. I want you to finish that by the time I bring the soup. OK?

Gideon does not move. She goes back into the kitchen.

MARK: Do you know what it's like to be worshipped by a saint? She truly believed that I – this object in front of you – because a writer, was actually *better*, actually superior to her, mere creature of instinct! What could I do? I encouraged her. I got her to regard herself as entirely frivolous. Trivial! Unworthy of her important husband! . . . And the more she cringed in awe, the more I hated her . . . Well, naturally . . .

He goes to the bed, snatches up the bottle, and drinks.

My Son-Confessor. You were never fooled. You saw him only too clear: the killer in me. It's why I had to get rid of you. You knew how he'd finish the brandy alone at night in the villa – then stand in the bathroom, sticking pins of seconal into his face, saying: 'Let this be the Young! The hateful Young!' How he'd tear his own hair in front of the mirror – hit himself with his own construction worker's hand, screaming inside: 'Why was I born without joy? Why do others have

it, and not me?' [*Softer*] And later, lying beside her in morning light, watching her wake. The only girl I ever knew who smiled first thing on waking. Watching the smile come, a second before the eyes open. Spill over me their bright love . . . Watching her in such anger.
> *Pause.*

Till one morning, she doesn't smile. She groans instead. One morning – after one particular night.
> *He turns away. Gideon begins to murmur below. He is very disturbed.*

GIDEON: [*low*] No one.

MARK: And I've got to . . . tell you . . .
> *He sits on the bed.*

GIDEON: No one and nothing . . . Just words . . . Words and nothing.

MARK: How does a dancer die, who doesn't want to live?

GIDEON: No! . . .

MARK: I watched my hate creep up her legs. It was as if I was needling it into her veins.

GIDEON: Theories . . . Lovely theories . . .

MARK: She goes to bed. The hips suddenly won't move. Don't want to any more.

GIDEON: [*agitated: half to himself*] Well, what else could I *do*? Join in? Bang, bang! 'Get out. Shrivings can't cope with you!' – is that what you want? . . . 'Stop it,' you say. 'Stop the voice!' Alright! That's easy to say. The hard thing is *not to*! Let it go on! Let it die of itself. Can't you see that? *It must die of itself*!
> *He springs up and starts pacing the room, speaking feverishly.*

The hard thing is to do nothing. Almost impossible . . . Well, we've spoken of it often enough . . . Answer me this! How could we throw him out, and live here afterwards ourselves? Doesn't it – in the end – doesn't it just – *just* – come down to *that*? To the sheer impossibility of that? . . . In the end, to shift at all – make any change that *is* a change – to *shove*, if you like, evolution on – and that's the task: no less! – *there have to be priorities*! . . . Alright. Abstraction! That's

just another bogey word! . . . I'm talking about a new kind of honour. Holding on to priorities. Do you see? . . .
He continues to walk up and down the room, hands clasped, caged in pain.
MARK: Finally, nothing moves. Except her mouth, praying. Just sits there in a canvas jacket, praying.
GIDEON: Yes . . . *Exactly*! . . . That's what's needed . . . A new kind of *honour* . . .
MARK: Shoving the book under the pillow whenever she hears me coming. 'Sorry, Gesù! Must go now! *He* won't understand!'
GIDEON: When we say Faith, it's *that* . . . What is worth honouring? Really worth it? . . . Really? . . . *Really?*
He stops short.
You real people, what will you really honour?
MARK: [*shouting at the shrine*] Oh you martyrs! You martyrs!
He springs to his feet and over to the shrine.
Why couldn't you ever fight me like a woman?
GIDEON: [*rapidly*] You speak of love all the time. But what will you honour? . . . Everyone says Love: you've got to fight for your love. Alright! But what does that mean? Do you think silence can't be fight? Do you judge a love only by the *bashing* you do for it? [*Bitterly*] Oh yes! Stand up! Square up! Come outside! Come on the battlefield! History of the World! Put your fists where your faith is! Marvellous! . . . [*Harshly*] And that's what you want too, with all your long hair, sweet looks! . . . All of you, just the same . . .
Pause. He stands for a moment, with eyes closed.
[*Quieter: very calm*] To let go. Just to let go that *indulgence*. Fill up instead with true passiveness. A feeling so total, it's *like* violence. An immense Nothing inside you. A sledge-hammer Nothing which alone can break that crust of Ego . . . Fasts – Vigils – all those tricks: what are they about, except this? – to fill up in a new way!
Pause. He stands very still, like a statue.
You have to stand there, my dear, and take it. Bang – and no reply. None. [*Dead*] None. None . . .

He starts to tremble. Suddenly he begins to imitate himself, in a new and bitter, spinsterish voice.
'Be quiet, Mark, please. Be silent, Mark. Mark, I forbid you. Mark, I beg you.' [*Savagely*] Words! Words and nothing! Lovely nothing! [*Crying out*] Oh, David!
MARK: [*standing before the shrine: low*] Giulia!
GIDEON: *David!*
MARK: My dancer!
GIDEON: *David! My David! . . . My owl . . . .*
Lois comes in with a bowl of steaming soup. She stares at Gideon. He becomes aware of her. Slowly he sits again at the table. She places the soup in front of him.
LOIS: Eat.
He does not move, or look at her.
Eat, Giddy. [*Pause*] Look, if you're mad at me, OK let me have it. Anything but the noble act. Sitting there all wounded. That's just shit, Giddy.
He remains motionless, as do Father and son above.
OK, I did it! So what does that make me? A Scarlet Woman? . . . OK, say it, if that's what you think. And it is exactly what you think! Only it's too aggressive to say it right out, isn't it? . . . Wow!
Pause.
Gee, I'm disappointed in you. Who'd have thought that you, of all people in the world, would be jealous? Anything so *ordinary*! . . . Sagging Jesus, as my lover would say! . . . Well, you live and learn. Or do you? I don't learn a damn thing, except that everyone's full of shit, and that's not much to learn. Every classroom cynic you meet in college tells you that. It's funny to find out they're right. That's funny . . .
Pause.
Say something, for Christ's sake! Who d'you think you are, some kind of a priest or something? Mark's right – he's absolutely right! It's the Pope! I've offended the Pope! The lowly acolyte has displeased the Pope of Reason! [*Mock humble*] Alright, I did it, Your Holiness. I have sinned. I did it, Your Holiness. I have sinned. I did it. So what? [*Angry*] Sex, sex, sex! So what? Supposed to be so great! What's

great? *He's* the famous lover – he didn't find it great. It took him forever! Just a fat old man, dropping his sweat on me! And that's supposed to be beautiful! . . . *What are they all lying about?*
> *Pause. Still Gideon does not move.*

MARK: [*softly*] Perdonna. Perdonna me. Perdonna.
> *Lois laughs.*

LOIS: No, that's not why you're angry, is it? It's not the fuck, is it? It's him! The Enemy! I went off with the Opposition! [*False English accent*] 'Isn't that the end, my deah? She doesn't do it for two whole years, and when she *does,* who does she choose? A nice Progressive fuck with an approved young boy? Oh no. She has to have a beastly, reactionary fuck with his old man!' [*She laughs: then coolly*] You don't care at all, do you? I'm kidding. I know it's not jealousy. It's nothing. It's absolutely nothing – right? You don't give a damn who I go to bed with! As far as you are concerned, I could go to bed with Hitler! . . . [*She laughs*] Boy, you really are a mess! I mean it. Like you sit there with your nose up in the air, preaching all the time – Non-attachment – Get Beyond the Possessive Scene – all that beautiful new humanist shit! – and all there is is *you,* making a great Cause out of not caring. A way of life, yeah, a whole religion – out of not feeling anything personal at all! [*She comes closer*] I saw you last night, when he attacked me. Oh, you were distressed, alright. It was a distressing scene. Difficult to handle, even for a saint. But you managed. You managed, Giddy. You handled it OK! [*Grandly*] 'Come, Lois. I am tireder than I thought.' [*Pause. Coldly*] You bastard.
> *He looks at her in amazement. She speaks with deep hostility.*

I think you actually enjoyed it. Like it was a test of your virtue. 'Poor Lois. Horrid for her, of course: but good for her too. You gotta be tested, after all. Everyone's got to be tested?' Right? Just stand there and take it. Right . . . [*Leaning into his face*] *Isn't that right?*
> *Gideon puts his hands over his ears and turns away from her. For a second she falters and stops.*

MARK: [*dead*] Alright. Let me give it to you in the face. How I actually killed her, your mother. How I actually finished her off. Short and physical.

LOIS: At least, he knows! He's the filthiest man I've met, but he knows something!

MARK: One night . . .

LOIS: He's not a phoney.

MARK: One night . . .

LOIS: He's garbage, but at least he's not a complete phoney.

MARK: [*with sudden violence*] Take your eyes off me! Get out of here! I can't speak!

He turns away.

LOIS: [*now relentless*] Do you know what a phoney is, Giddy? A person who says the family is obsolete, and all he really wishes is that David Askelon was his own son!

Gideon turns to look at her.

Do you know what a phoney is? Someone who says Peace because there's no war in him. I don't mean he drove it out – I mean he never had it. It's easy to be chaste when you've got no cock, Giddy. It's easy to give up bloodshed, if you've got no blood to shed! Right? Dig that! I made an epigram! You see, I'm not so pompous as everyone says! . . . [*Icy*] You know something? I don't believe your word on anything. Like when you say when you were young, you were attracted to boys and dogs and shit knows what? I tell you, I don't believe a fucking word. *I think you're exactly like me. You can't stand it!* You made that whole thing up just to teach a point. [*English accent*] 'Sex Freedom is a jolly good thing!' But I'm willing to bet my ass you never did it at all. Everyone says how noble you were to give it up – just *imagine* what he went through to do it! . . . Well, yeah, I can imagine. It was like nothing! No wonder she left you, your wife. No wonder she just got out, poor stupid Enid. She found out what a phoney she was hitched to. What a phoney! Christ, at least he's alive up there! Not dead – as good as dead! – Dead thing! Dead old thing! Dead! Boring – dead! – ridiculous – Dead! phoney – Dead! – old – dead! dead! dead! DEAD!

Deliberately, Gideon strikes her as she leans over him.

*She recoils. He rises. She retreats. He strikes her again
more violently. She stares at him in horror.*
Pause.
GIDEON: Are you satisfied? In your deep heart, are you satisfied?
*She turns from him. Then he turns from her. They stand
frozen.*
Pause.
MARK: [*flatly*] One night. She lying upstairs: I below, turning
over my book of love poems. I get up. I drive into town. I sit
in the arcade. I see a girl. I signal. I drive her back to the villa.
I go up with her, into your mother's room. She lying there,
drinking coca-cola her favourite way, out of the bottle. Now
barely able to speak, she turns to me with her usual smile for
any new thing. The girl giggles. 'Don't be afraid,' I say. 'My
wife enjoys this. It's for her we do it.' [*Pause*] And so. Slowly.
On the floor. At the foot of the bed from which she could not
move. I saluted her with my ecstasies. [*Pause*] During the
whole time she held the bottle before her, as if she were
offering me refreshment. It was next morning she groaned
first thing on waking. Very exactly: once. As if she were
clearing her throat. [*Pause*] She didn't live three weeks after
that. I remember she held the cola bottle night and day. Like
a doll to a sick child.
*Silence. Then David moves, quickly. His hands fly up,
join violently above his head. For a long moment they
stay up there, poised to smash his father down. Then he
begins to tremble. Slowly his arms are lowered over his
father's head. He pulls Mark to him, and kisses him on
the face. They stay still.*
Below neither Lois nor Gideon moves.
LOIS: [*low*] Don't ever forgive me.
*David releases Mark. He moves, and shuts the shrine on
his mother's image.*
Don't ever.
DAVID: Go down to him.
MARK: No.
DAVID: You *have* to.
MARK: You. You're his son where it matters.

DAVID: No. You are. [*Pause*] Padre.

MARK: Figlio.

> *They stare at each other.*

DAVID: Va.

MARK: Si.

> *Mark leaves the bedroom, and comes slowly downstairs.*
> *David sits on the bed, exhausted.*

LOIS: [*quietly*] That night we met in jail. I was reading John Stuart Mill. Where he asked himself that question: if all the wrongs in the world were put right, would you yourself be any happier? – and the answer came back No. You said, for you it would be Yes. [*Pause*] I never heard anything better than that.

> *She turns and sees Mark watching them both. He moves towards them. She ignores him, and walks straight by him up the stairs. Gideon does not move. The girl hesitates outside the bedroom door – looks in – sees David – enters. David does not look at her.*
> *Pause.*

MARK: [*seeing the bowl of soup*] You haven't even eaten.

LOIS: Hey.

DAVID: Hay is for horses.

LOIS: Sure.

MARK: I warned you. I did. [*With fury*] You talk about life! –

> *Lois turns her face to the wall, but does not leave.*

No. *We* talk about life – the knowers. And look at us. You are the only possible thing I've ever met. D'you wonder I hate you?

DAVID: [*woodenly*] Why, Lois?

MARK: D'you wonder I love you?

DAVID: Why?

LOIS: [*as woodenly*] I don't know.

DAVID: Did you enjoy it, at least?

LOIS: [*quietly: with absolute frankness*] I don't know what enjoy means.

MARK: I wish I was an animal, and could live without a dream. I wish I was a child, and could live in a Church. But I'm a man, and I've known you. Where else can I go?

LOIS: I don't know who I am, David.
*Mark moves forward and thrusts his outstretched hand
before the motionless Gideon.*
MARK: Here! This. This tool for making. A killer's hand.
It's all you've got . . . Take it.
Gideon ignores it, staring straight ahead.
What will it do without you? Squeeze some more napalm out
of my cock? Drive some more Red tanks over dreaming heads?
Wear the Pope's ring, and dip a gold pen in the sick of starving
children it's helped create. Sign me Governor of Louisibama,
and decree at parties for the blind, white guests must be
separated from black by charitable hands, since they can't
see to do God's work for themselves. Don't leave me with
this God's hand, Giddy.
LOIS: [*quietly*] I'm no place, David. No place at all.
DAVID: Shrivings is a place.
LOIS: No.
DAVID: It has to be.
LOIS: It's nowhere.
DAVID: [*violently*] It has to be! IT HAS TO BE!
*The girl turns. He turns round to her. They stare at one
another.*
MARK: Have you no word for me? No word at all?
GIDEON: Dust.
*Appalled, Mark sits down at the table. He takes up a
spoon. He dips it in the soup, and presents it to Gideon.*
MARK: Peace!
*Gideon sits rigid.
Above, David suddenly stretches out his arm to Lois.
She looks at it without expression: motionless.
A long pause.
Then, very slowly, Gideon begins to lower his head to the
spoon held before him. He does not look at Mark. He
opens his mouth, and drinks.
The light fades.*

CURTAIN

PETER SHAFFER was born in Liverpool, England, in 1926. During the Second World War he worked as a conscript in a coal mine; later he studied history on a scholarship to Cambridge University, and departed thence to New York, concerning which city he had long entertained an obsessive and glittering fantasy. There he worked in a Doubleday bookstore, and the Forty-second Street library, living for much of the time in Hell's Kitchen, and returning three years later to London convinced of his own unemployability. In some desperation he wrote his first play, *Five Finger Exercise,* which was produced in 1958 to widespread approval (in New York in 1959, to ditto), thereby relieving him of the necessity of working in other stores or offices.

The success of his first play suggested to Mr. Shaffer that he might be a dramatist at heart. Partly because he had no aptitude for doing anything else, he sat down during the ensuing years and produced other plays. All of these met with great success, first in London and then in New York: *The Private Ear* and *The Public Eye,* a double bill, in 1962; *The Royal Hunt of the Sun,* an epic concerning the conquest of Peru, which Bernard Levin described as "the greatest play of our generation," in 1964; and in the following year *Black Comedy,* a romp designed for Britain's National Theatre, which another critic hailed as "the farce of the century."

Peter Shaffer is based in London, but tries to spend several months each year in New York, being still entirely possessed of his fantasy concerning her, and now knowing with his eyes, ears and inwards that she is the most beautiful and dreadful city on earth.